Spinning for Salmon

Spinning for Salmon

Gary Webster

ROBERT HALE · LONDON

© Gary Webster 2010
First published in Great Britain 2010

ISBN 978-0-7090-9017-5

Robert Hale Limited
Clerkenwell House
Clerkenwell Green
London EC1R 0HT

www.halebooks.com

A catalogue record for this book is available from the British Library

2 4 6 8 10 9 7 5 3 1

Typeset in 10/12.7pt Palatino
Printed in Great Britain by
MPG Books Group, Bodmin and King's Lynn

Contents

Acknowledgements

What I know about taking salmon on spinning gear I learned from countless hours on the water. From fishing, sure, but just as much from other fishers I've met along the way: talking to them, trading stories, even secrets, sometimes just standing back and watching. They have been my best teachers, and it's to them that I owe my first debt of gratitude – for their patience, trust, and good-natured comradeship. A few deserve special thanks: Stig and Renée Höglund, for showing me how deep-sweeping ought to be done; the late Micke H., for lessons on how to rip and take the occasional warmer-water salmon; Ingvar, for showing me just how good you can get at harling; and Bakhir, for general spooning tips. I also want to thank Mike Taylor, proprietor of the Red Lion Hotel on the River Wye at Bredwardine, for sharing his years of experience on rigging up and fishing Wye minnows.

A number of researchers also deserve my thanks for letting me pick their brains for insights on salmon behaviour. Dr Laura Weir let me in on her still unpublished findings on adult/parr salmon interactions. Several others helped me with the question of salmon running depths, by sharing observations, hunches and research findings, and by pointing me to helpful publications: Dr Jon Svedsen, Dr Morten Stickler, Dr Petri Karppinen, Dr Panu Orell, Dr Saija Koljonen, Dr Øyvind Garmo, Dr Peter Rivinoja, Dr Frode Oppedal, Dr Eva Thorstad and Dr Eli Kvingedal. Several others helped me sort out some snaggy questions about salmonid vision: Dr Indigo Novales Flamarigue, Dr Robert Batty, Dr Craig Hawryshyn, Dr Deborah Stenkamp, Dr Peter Wainwright and Dr Elianne Lundmark.

Thanks also to Tommy Engström and Daniel Almgren of Cykel & Fiskecenter, Skellefteå (www.cykelochfiskecenter.se), for keeping me in the loop with angling news and for giving me free run of the place for shooting tackle photos. Thanks, too, to Jokke Kerttula of Kert's Fiske & Fritid (www.kertsfiske.se) in Skelleftehamn for doing the same.

Diagrams 19a–f reprinted from *Spin-Fishing for Sea Trout* by Gary Webster with the kind permission of Crowood Press.

Introduction

The Atlantic salmon is known as the king of freshwater game fish. Most anglers agree. Those that don't have probably never hooked a fresh-run 20 lb (9 kg) fish on a warm August evening. What's it like? Let's say something between hanging on to a rocket and a missile! Unforgettable, anyway. Pound for pound, this has to be the toughest fighting fish you'll hook in fresh water. Also the most exasperating – some days almost too easy to catch, other days impossible. Someone once said that long experience brings trout anglers mastery and salmon anglers humility. I've always taken that as a challenge.

Mention salmon fishing, and most people picture fishermen standing waist deep whipping colourful flies across the water with fifteen-foot rods. True, the salmon has long been the supreme trophy of the fly angler, and on many rivers fly-fishers do take a lot of fish. But the fact is, spinning anglers often take just as many, and on some rivers even more.[1]

Now, the fly-fisher interested in reading up on how the experts do it has a ton of books to choose from. Good luck to the spinner looking for some guidance on how to take salmon on hardware, though. To be sure, most salmon angling books devoted to fly-fishing also have a chapter on spinning, but the treatment is nearly always fairly thin. Even the great all-round salmon anglers presented spinning as something you did when conditions weren't good enough for fly-fishing.

Who knows why spin-fishing for salmon hasn't carved out its own place in the angling literature? Spinning baits have certainly been around long enough. In his book *Salmon Fishing* (1984) Hugh Falkus mentioned a 1,100-year-old reference to a

Danish angler fishing a 'lure of bryte shel' – sounds like an early spoon to me. By the late 1800s salmon anglers were casting, jigging (called *trolling* or *trowling*) and harling (called *trailing* then) spinning baits with rods armed with primitive centre-pin and fixed-spool reels – precursors to today's multipliers and spinning reels.[2]

Now, don't get me wrong: the hardware angler can learn a lot about taking salmon from the fly-fisher. I've incorporated some of it here. But spinning for salmon has a rich tradition too, with much to learn. Just like the fly-fishers, generations of spinners have left us hundreds of lures to choose from, dozens of presentations to master and a wealth of know-how about rods, reels, lines and other tackle. There is also a whole body of hard-won insights into salmon taking behaviour and how to make the right tactical decisions at the waterside to cash in on it with spinning gear.

Enough said. That's what this manual is intended to do: present what's known about how to hook, play and land salmon on spinning tackle. The focus is on the Atlantic salmon (*Salmo salar*) and on catching them in rivers. Atlantic salmon because that's our (European) native fish, and because that's where my own experience lies. Atlantics are also found in North America all along the north-eastern coast. But American anglers have other salmon to choose from as well, like the King or Chinook, Silver or Coho, Chum, Sockeye, and Pink. These are found mostly in Pacific Coast rivers from California to Alaska, with a few new introductions into some north-eastern rivers and even some European waters. Some of the methods I'll be talking about were first developed on Pacific Coast rivers. I've included them because they seem to work just as well on European waters.

I'm well aware that some anglers fish for Atlantics in still water – both fresh and salt – as well as in rivers. So why my focus on river salmon only? First, that's where most anglers fish for them. Second, catching migrating salmon more interested in spawning than hunting for food presents a special kind of angling challenge. Stillwater boat anglers have different challenges, and they've addressed these with a pretty specialized repertoire of deep-trolling gear: they deserve their own manual.[3]

How This Manual Is Put Together

Those who have read my *Spin-Fishing for Sea Trout* (Crowood Press, 2008) will notice that this manual is laid out in much the same fashion. I planned it that way, for two reasons. The first is so you can make easy comparisons. Most salmon anglers also fish for sea trout. In Europe at least most waters hold both kinds of fish, and it's not uncommon to hook both on the same day. Some spinning anglers are happy to fish non-selectively – pot luck style – and take whichever fish happens along. But, if you're serious about taking salmon, you can do a lot better than that.

True, sea trout and salmon are very similar in many ways. They are often found in the same pieces of water and will take the very same lures, presented in the very same ways. But salmon aren't sea trout. They are different enough that choices about which presentations to use, and where and when to use them, can mean the difference between taking the occasional salmon and taking salmon when you want to, or at least more consistently.

The second reason for this layout is that I think the approach taken to spinning for sea trout works for salmon too: you start with the fish and work back to the fisher. So this manual starts out by looking at the nature of our quarry: the river salmon. It covers what it's like physically, its life history and why and how it takes a lure. Chapter 2 deals with lures: why some lures work better than others, how a lure's effectiveness is influenced by things like water clarity and light levels, and how you can make smart choices among the wide range of spinning baits available.

Chapter 3 deals with the best ways to deliver a lure into the strike zone depending on the kind of water you are fishing and whether you are working on foot or from a harling boat; also with the kinds of tackle set-ups and rigging you'll need to do it. It also describes how to deal with a salmon once you've managed to hook it – how to play it and land it.

I want to say straight off that, although I've caught my share of salmon over the years, I don't consider myself in the same league as some of the one hundred plus fish-per-year anglers I've known and fished alongside. But I have learned a lot from them. So, even though I've never been able to make all of their techniques work as well for me as they do for them, I've included as many as I can here – along with my own bread-and-butter moves. Some will perhaps be old news to experienced sea trout fishers, but others won't.

Chapter 4 deals with tactics. It covers in some detail how to read the water, how to locate likely salmon lies and how to choose the best lures and presentations for covering fish. I end the chapter by sketching out how I'd go about fishing a piece of river under the different conditions you're likely to encounter.

As in *Spin-Fishing for Sea Trout*, many of the points made in the text are tied to endnotes, where you can find a little more detail, as well as links to their sources (which are all listed in the Bibliography). I've added an Appendix that gives guidelines for anybody interested in making some of their own salmon lures. Throughout the manual you'll also find boxes with extra information, tackle tips and lists of good lure choices.

What about bait-fishing? Many anglers fish natural baits – like shrimp, squid, herring and worms, etc. – off spinning rigs for salmon. Bait-fishing has a long and rich tradition, with pretty specialized and sophisticated techniques for preparing, mounting and delivering baits effectively. I'm not much of a bait angler. Even if I were, I couldn't do it justice in a manual of this size, so I'm not even going to try. Instead, I've included some of the ways natural baits and scents can be used to increase the effectiveness of hardware lures (see 'How about Smell?' on p. 54)

Stealth, Confidence and Persistence

Some new anglers may think that getting good at catching salmon is about learning the mechanics. Certainly that's a big part of it. But one of the things that separates great salmon fishers from the rest is attitude. So, before going any further, a few thoughts about getting into the right frame of mind for taking salmon.

Hugh Falkus listed three keys to success as a salmon angler: stealth, confidence and persistence (*Salmon Fishing*, p. 35). I'll leave stealth for a later chapter. As for confidence, this is basic to all angling success. If you have confidence in a lure, then you fish it better and you catch more fish. Same goes for presentations, tackle, the rest. Lack of confidence only brings hesitation, disrupts concentration and leads to random chucking instead of targeted casting, and to a lot of wasted water-time changing lures.

You build confidence one lure at a time, one fish at a time, until you've got an arsenal of moves you know you can count on. For many this takes a lifetime of trial and error. One of the objectives of a manual like this is to bring together a good collection of tried-and-trues (lures, presentations, tackle set-ups) that will serve as a base on which to build a confident approach to spin-fishing for salmon.

Persistence is also important, especially when it comes to river salmon. These fish aren't looking for a meal; they won't clamour to get at something you've tossed at them. For every salmon that slams a lure, maybe twenty others let it pass by.[4] To be a consistent scorer in salmon fishing you've got to play the percentages.

My objective every time I go out is to see how many salmon I can cover. I figure the more fish I can tick off in a day by putting a lure in their face, the better my chances that one will take me up on the challenge. I might not end up going home with a fish. But at least I'll know I had a fighting chance. Since I'm not very patient by nature, keeping that objective in mind – covering fish – keeps me focused and keeps me going until one does take my lure.

To stealth, confidence and persistence, I want to add another key to success: mission. In *Spin-Fishing for Sea Trout* I talk about the importance of setting goals. It's just as basic to success in salmon angling. First, it's important to understand that successful salmon anglers are successful because that's what they *want* to be. It doesn't just happen, and it isn't about luck. They've worked for it – if you can call fishing work. They catch more salmon because that's their mission.

Don't laugh. Catching lots of salmon isn't the primary goal of every angler. People fish for a lot of reasons: to get away, to be close to nature, to find peace and quite, to meet buddies at the riverside – and if they catch the odd fish, all the better. If that's your idea of fishing you probably don't need a manual like this. All you need to do is pop into the nearest tackle shop, ask them to fit you out with the tackle you need and show you how to use it. Let them point you in the direction of the best beats, and before too long you'll be pulling out the occasional salmon like any average angler.

But if you want to catch more salmon than that; if you want to catch them consistently; if you want to catch them under a whole range of conditions; or if you want to catch them when other rods aren't; and if you care about doing that more than about nature, peace-and-quiet or waterside socializing, then this manual will help.

Now, let's take a look at our quarry.

1. Our Quarry: The Atlantic Salmon (*Salmo salar*)

Just watch a salmon jumping up through some rapids (or, better yet, on the end of your line), and you know you're dealing with a high-performance fish. The ancient Romans were impressed when they first caught sight of Atlantic salmon making their way up British rivers and tagged them *salmo* – which literally means 'the fish that leaps'. And do they ever! Jumps of five or six feet are common, and a vertical leap of twelve feet was measured over the Orrin Falls in Scotland (Falkus, 1984, p. 35). Pound for pound, the Atlantic salmon is probably the strongest fish in the river. The fastest too, clocking some 13 ft (4 m)/sec in a sprint. That's more than 9 mph (14.5 kmph)![5]

But high performance demands high-quality water. So we tend to find Atlantics in the cool, clean, well-oxygenated streams and rivers of the north.[6] That's also where we find their closest relatives, the sea-run brown trout or sea trout (*Salmo trutta*) and all the Pacific Coast salmon, the King (Chinook), Silver (Coho), Chum, Sockeye and Pink. Native populations of Atlantics are found throughout northern Europe in coastal rivers south to the Massif Central in France and across the Atlantic from northern Quebec down to Connecticut. In the last century Atlantic salmon were successfully introduced to New Zealand, Australia, Argentina and Chile.

Life Cycle

I guess most anglers have a rough idea of the salmon's life history. For those who don't, here's the short version. It all starts in the shallow headwaters of some clean freshwater stream. Sometime between November and January the hen fish lays up to 100,000 eggs in a kind of nest she's made or 'cut' with her tail in the gravel. This is usually in a foot or two of fairly fast, clear, flowing water; it's about a yard across and called a redd. After the male or cock fish fertilizes the eggs by spraying milt (semen) over them, the hen swims up a little ahead and covers the eggs with smaller gravel, again using her tail. After several months the embryos grow into little fish called alevins, with egg sacs still attached that supply them with about a month's worth of nutrition. Once the sac is spent, the alevins swim away from the nest and, as small fry or parr salmon, start hunting small invertebrates. Parr can be identified by the distinctive 'finger marks' along their flanks.[7]

Parr stay in fresh water anywhere from two to four years and grow to be about 12 in (30 cm) long by living off mainly larvae, nymphs and small shellfish. Curiously, some male parr actually reach sexual maturity at this stage. These precocious cocks are sometimes called sneakers because they compete with the big males at spawning time by sneaking under them to fertilize the ripe eggs. It's a dangerous business, though. Both the big cocks and hens often attack and injure them (see Gage *et al.*). But apparently it's worth it; on some rivers parr make major contributions to fatherhood.[8] As spinners we can learn much from sneakers about how to design and fish lures effectively – more on that later.

At Sea

Before parr can migrate to sea, they need to develop salt-secreting cells in their gills; they also lose the finger marks, become silvery and turn into slender little fish we call smolts. Once transformed, they head downriver into the estuary and out into the open sea – usually with the first spring floods. Most salmon spend several years out in the salt water, hunting schools of herring, capelin, sprats, sand eels, whiting and other pelagic creatures.

All European and American salmon feed and mingle in the North Atlantic from the pack ice off Greenland, north to the Barents Sea and east to the North Sea and the southern Baltic. Life at sea is dangerous. Predators take a heavy toll – up to ninety per cent of the smolts. But the remainder grow to maturity to return to their natal rivers to spawn. Some do this after only one year at sea as small salmon of under 10 lb (4.5 kg), called grilse. But most stay out for another year or so, even up to four before returning as large maiden salmon weighing 20–50 lb (9–22.5 kg). It's apparently all done by smell: returning salmon have the scent of their natal rivers imprinted during their early freshwater years. Migrating back they wander along the coast and with sea currents, sometimes even exploring estuaries, until they pick up the familiar scent and home in on it. Most seem to find their way back. Some don't, and end up spawning in foreign waters. Once in an estuary they will pause for a time – days to weeks – to adjust physiologically to the sweet water again, and to wait for a sufficient flow to run upriver, often with high or ebbing tides and usually at night (see Karppinen *et al.*). That's where *we* wait for them.

River Returns

Like sea trout, salmon tend to move upriver in step-like waves or runs (Finstad *et al.*). Most rivers get at least a couple of distinct runs each year, some more. In British waters the major runs are in spring and autumn. The bigger fish come first – the so-called springers. These are in peak physical condition, bright silver, and considered by many to be the cream of salmon fishing. The fall runners are usually smaller and include many one-sea-year grilse.

The exact timing of the runs varies much from one location to another. Assessing when, how long and even if salmon will run up any particular river is a matter of local knowledge. But as Hugh Falkus pointed out in *Salmon Fishing*, 'By selecting his rivers, an angler with the time and money to spare could be salmon fishing somewhere in Britain or Ireland for the full eleven months of the year' (1984, p. 67). Weather can also knock a normal schedule off, one way or the other. Salmon have a hard time negotiating fast water or obstacles when the water dips below 41°F (5°C), so a really cold spring can stall an early run until it warms a little. Same when the water is very low or gets very warm, say above 68°F (20°C), like during a really hot 'Indian' summer when fish will wait for higher, cooler water to migrate (Dahl *et al.*).

As spawning time approaches, fish lose their bright shiny silver appearance, taking on a darker reddish-orange 'plumage'. The males also develop a pronounced hook to the lower jaw, called a kype. After spawning, a salmon is emaciated and weak; many are also battered and scarred from fighting. But, unlike their Pacific Coast cousins, most don't die. Many of the females, at least, survive to spawn three, even four times. We call each year's spawned-out fish kelts. Some will make their way back to the sea right away to start eating and repairing. Some will over-winter in the lower reaches of the river and follow the spring floods out to sea. I hook a number of them each year while fishing for late-winter sea trout.

Size

So how big a fish are you likely to hook into on the river? That's going to depend a lot on the river. Generally speaking, rod-caught Atlantics will run from about 5–20 lb (2.3–9 kg) with most in the 10–12 lb (4.5–5.5 kg) range. But there are much bigger trophies out there. Most rivers in Britain report fish of 20 lb (9 kg) or more caught each year. And probably everybody's heard of the current British record fish, which weighed 64 lb (29 kg), taken by the Scottish ghillie's daughter Miss Georgina Ballantine one October dusk while trolling a natural dace 'minnow' in the Boat Pool at Murthly, on the Glendelvine beat of the River Tay, in 1922. The monster was 54 in (137 cm) long, 28½ in (72 cm) around, and took two hours and a half mile of river to land![9] A few years back, the *Daily Mail* (16 October 2007) reported what was probably an even bigger catch on the River Ness. This was a big male in full spawning colours that measured 56 in (142 cm) long and 50 in (127 cm) round. Too bad it was returned before it could be weighed. But, judging by the dimensions, it probably tipped 100 lb (45 kg).

Know your salmon from your sea trout

Save embarrassment when it's bragging time, maybe even a stiff fine for taking an out-of-season fish. Learn how to tell the difference between a salmon and a sea trout. Here are the distinguishing features:

Size: Salmon are bigger. Typical salmon caught weighs about 10 lb (4.5 kg); typical sea trout less than half that.

Body shape: Salmon are more slender and streamlined; sea trout broader and stockier.

Markings: Salmon have fewer and smaller spots or flecks and most are above the lateral line; sea trout typically have larger spots and more below the lateral line.

Tail wrist: Salmon have a thin tail wrist (caudal peduncle) that makes a nice handle for tailing a fish to land it; a sea trout's tail wrist is too thick to provide a good grip.

Mouth: A salmon's mouth is smaller so the jaw line just reaches to the eye; a sea trout's jaw line reaches a little past the eye.

Tail shape: The salmon's tail is always forked; a mature sea trout's tail is squared off.

Scale count: Salmon have fewer scales so they feel rougher than sea trout. If you count the number of scales running in

---

a diagonal line between the rear of the adipose fin and the lateral line you'll find between ten and twelve, usually eleven, on a salmon, and thirteen to sixteen, usually fourteen, on a sea trout.

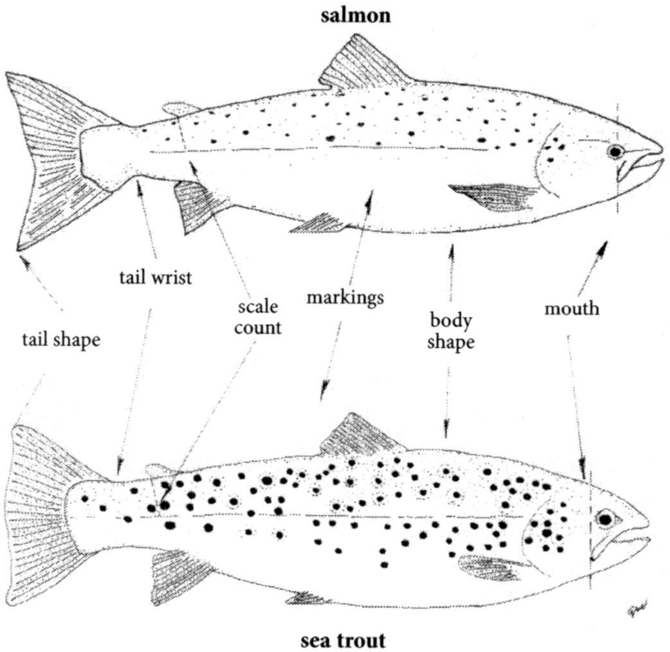

salmon

tail wrist

scale
count

markings

body
shape

mouth

tail shape

sea trout

Physical differences between salmon and sea trout.

Why and How Salmon Strike

Salmon, like sea trout, stop eating once they enter fresh water. This kind of anorexia seems to be triggered by both water temperature and the fish's sexual maturity (see Kadri *et al.*). So, if it's true that salmon stop eating once back in the river, why do we bother trying to catch them at all? Good question. The fact is, the fast isn't total. Some fish do continue to consume food from time to time, especially females that haven't yet fattened up sufficiently for the hardships of spawning. As for the rest, this anorexia translates to an aversion to *swallowing* things, although not necessarily to grabbing them. And that, after all, is what we want to make salmon do: *grab* our lures, not eat them!

Salmon might strike for any number of reasons other than hunger. Basic instinct is one: as in other predatory fish, the strike reflex is highly developed in salmon. Anything lifelike that enters the salmon's personal space may elicit an instantaneous strike reaction. You can see it any warm summer's evening on the river: salmon after salmon (sea trout too) rising to snatch tiny creatures, even occasional flotsam from the surface. Yet, when we catch these same fish and cut them open, their stomachs are almost always empty. These fish are reflex-striking, not feeding.

Moreover, experience has taught us that there are certain kinds of actions or movements that seem to trigger a strike reaction more than others. An object suddenly appearing or streaking overhead, or one that darts up and away – movements similar to insects or escaping fish – will often elicit a strike response. So will a slow wobbling action – maybe something like a wounded and vulnerable bait-fish would have. We want to work these actions and movements into our repertoire of lures and presentations.

We know, too, that salmon will strike out of aggression. They are highly territorial, and prime lies are fought for and defended. How large a personal space a salmon is willing to defend isn't certain. But based on anglers' observations it's probably inside a radius of about 6 ft (1.8 m), about the same as a salmon's *reaction distance* or strike zone (see Chapter 3). Any intruder to that space, whether another fish or a lure, risks being attacked and expelled. It's not surprising that precocious parr salmon are frequent targets of such attacks. Hugh Falkus and his fishing buddies reported seeing this kind of aggression on their home rivers:

> One salmon I was watching grabbed a parr that by darting suddenly across his lie had (presumably) strayed too close. The little fish was seized broadside on with the front of the mouth, held for a moment or two while the salmon drifted backwards downstream, and then spat out. (Falkus, 1984, p. 54)

Most of the aggressive strikes are probably the result of sexual competition between adults and precocious sneaker parr. And it's not only the big males that attack – females do too, at least once spawning has actually begun. Fish biologist Laura Weir, who studies and even films these interactions, has been kind enough to describe them to me:

> Adult males do attack the parr, but interestingly females do it more frequently. In my experience, this occurs mostly during spawning, when the female is on her nest, the parr are behind her and the big males are around as well. I think the female attacks them because they are usually in the way of her making a nest, and she will get any part of them she can. We have found parr in female stomachs on a few occasions, likely as a result of a very successful attack.

Lesson: If mature fish will go after intrusive sneaker parr out of anger, why not lures that act the same? We've also learned from experience that an active fish is more likely to take a lure than one holding or resting calmly. It makes sense: moving fish encounter others, and agitation and aggression are heightened. It's not surprising if our lure is enough of an added irritation to elicit an attack. Falkus suggested that salmon will also strike out of curiosity, even playfulness – why not? (1984, p. 48)

Bottom line: Our success with salmon doesn't hinge on finding feeders, only on inducing fish to strike our lures. That's what we need to think about when choosing which lures to use and how to present them. The next two chapters will deal with just that.

2. Spinning Baits for Salmon

Artificial spinning baits have been around much longer, it seems, than anglers willing to try them on salmon. Apart from that 1,100-year-old reference to fishing with a 'lure of bryte shel' noted above, angling literature from the seventeenth century onwards is fairly crammed with descriptions of a range of hardware baits – primitive spoons and spinners – and how to use them on pike, trout, even perch. But not salmon! As late as 1726 George Smith could write in *The Gentleman Angler* (p. 38) that 'There are two ways of angling for salmon, either with the Artificial Fly, or with Bait', by which he meant specifically the lobworm, while in the very same volume giving detailed descriptions of artificial minnows.[10]

In fact, it's not until well into the nineteenth century that we find any evidence of a small – although by no means wholly accepted – cadre of salmon spinners. One of them, the angling author Edward Fitzgibbon (pen name Ephemera), noted it almost in passing in his book of 1865, *A Handbook of Angling Teaching Fly-Fishing, Trolling, Bottom-Fishing and Salmon-Fishing*: 'Salmon in my opinion and that of a few others may be frequently taken by spinning with a real bait or an *artificial one*'. Later in the same book he adds the recommendation that 'the best artificial fish-baits are those called "flexible", made by Mr Flinn, of Broad Street, Worcester' (pp. 160; 176).

The slow and relatively late acceptance and development of spinning as a method of taking river salmon would make a worthy study in its own right, but it is outside the scope of this manual. Suffice it to say here that by the close of the nineteenth century, spinners had fought and won a legitimate place alongside fly anglers on many if not most salmon rivers. Now, to more practical considerations.

What's a Good Salmon Lure?

I pretty much grew up in tackle shops. It seems hardly a week went by when my allowance wasn't spent on some colourful new lure for my bulging tackle box. If I remember right, only a few of them ever caught any fish, but I liked the look and feel of those shiny spoons, jewel-like spinners and glossy plugs. I still do, and it's probably as close as I can get to a reason for my preference for fishing hardware rather than flies.

I still haunt the local tackle shop. But I've learned to curb my kid-in-the-sweetshop impulses. Now, it's mainly news I'm after – who's catching what, when and how – and treble hooks for my own home-made lures. When I do buy a lure it's one I'm looking for specifically to fill a hole in my line-up of tried-and-trues. Over the years I've learned that, out of the wide range of lures available, you really need only a handful of different types and varieties to get you through a salmon season in good style.

So what should you look for in a spinning bait for salmon in rivers? Anglers differ, of course, on what they consider the most important salmon-catching features. But for me, and many successful salmon spinners I know, it comes down to something like the following half dozen or so qualities.

Deliverable Action

The great salmon and sea trout man Hugh Falkus once wrote: 'It is likely that a salmon can be caught on any object he can suck into his mouth. Tie a hook on a pencil-sharpener, fish it across the stream, and sooner or later a salmon will undoubtedly grab it' (1984, p. 326). True. But it's also true that one reason we don't spend much time fishing pencil-sharpeners is that a salmon is far more likely to grab a lure that has a good attractive action to it than one that doesn't.

So, first in importance for any good salmon spinning bait is what I call *deliverable action*. You want a lure you know you can deliver to the right depth and fish at the right speed, and that will also have the desired action when you do. Of course, this will depend on whether you want to fish it deep and slow or high and fast, and whether you are going to use it in strong currents, shallow riffles, gentle glides or lazy pools. But once you know where and how you want to present your lure then you can decide whether a spoon, a spinner, a plug or some other bait will do the trick in terms of deliverable action, and about how much it should weigh. It might be a heavy spoon or spinner, or a light and buoyant minnow or plug you've rigged up with weights, or maybe something else.

What kind of action should you look for? In my experience – both from fishing myself and from watching others who catch more than their fair share – the best salmon lures seem to have a *steady, rhythmic, lumbering action*. This is a different action from the one I want in my sea trout lures. For them, the more irregular, darting or frenzied the action the better, because that's what turns sea trout on. True, a sea trout lure will catch salmon too, but not as often as one with a steady, rhythmic, lumbering action. Why? No one knows for sure. Maybe it simulates a wounded herring or whiting or some other small fish salmon are only too happy to gobble up at sea, or maybe it's mistaken for one of those intrusive and irritating sneaker parr that adult salmon are forever trying to eradicate.

It might even be that a lure with a slower, rhythmic and predictable action is simply easier for a salmon to nail than a darting, erratic one. Underwater filming of feeding salmon tells us that salmon are surprisingly bad at actually catching prey fish (and lures). Professional North-American salmon troller Dick Pool routinely films happenings at the terminal tackle, and he reports that salmon will miss a lure two or three times before actually locking on. In one film, a fish hit the lure twenty-two times, before getting hooked on the twenty-third! He also filmed fish that, after bouts of repeatedly attacking and missing prey, followed them at a slower speed, sometimes for long distances, before eventually grabbing them by the tail.

What is certain is that a lure with good deliverable action attracts strikes for at least two reasons. First, it looks attractive. Second, it 'sounds' attractive. A moving, wobbling lure displaces water and gives off vibrations that salmon pick up through their lateral lines, the sense organs running the length of each of their sides. Dick Pool believes you can draw a salmon in from as far as 30 ft (9 m) by vibrations alone (www.protroll.com).

If you haven't guessed by now, salmon have pretty poor visual acuity compared with humans: they are great at detecting movement, contrasts, even subtle colour differences, but poor at detail. A lure – even at close range – appears blurry to them. So it's no surprise that a darting, erratic lure can often 'outmanoeuvre' a pursuing salmon. As I'll discuss below, some famous salmon lures like the Abu Toby have a reputation for being great at attracting strikes but poor at hooking fish for this very reason!

So deliverable action is a first consideration in a salmon lure: one with a steady, rhythmic action you can deliver to the right depth with the right speed (see Chapter 3). I'm pretty sure that if you chose lures on this feature alone – and forgot about size, colour and pattern altogether – you would probably catch more than your share of fish. Still, you can hedge your chances a little more if you look for some other features in a lure too.

Fish heavy and keep the rhythm

Some experts say always fish the lightest bait you can, and add weight to the line if you need to. This is good advice when you are looking to keep a lure fishing with a fast, erratic action: for example, when you're going after sea trout. But for salmon it's easier to keep the desired slow, steady, rhythmic action by fishing the heaviest lure you can for the conditions.

Lure Size

Lure size – by which I mean length – is probably the most important feature to look for in a salmon lure, next to action. Yet many spinning anglers don't think about this nearly enough. For many anglers the routine is to pull out their biggest sea trout lures (usually spoons and diving plugs in the 3–4 in (8–10 cm) range) and fish these right through the season. For years I did the same, and did pretty well too – at least once the water cooled down to under about 50°F (10°C); if it was much warmer, takes were more the exception than the norm.

Now I've learned what fly-fishers have long known, that salmon are much more likely to nail a smaller lure when the water is warm and a bigger lure when it's cold. No one can tell why, but it probably has to do with metabolism. Salmon are cold-blooded, which means their metabolic rate is directly tied to water temperature: the warmer the water, the higher the fish's metabolism and also its sensitivity to stimuli, like lures. In cold water it's the opposite. Hence, the big lure it takes to rouse the interest of a lethargic, cold-water fish is likely to turn off, or even spook, a keyed-up, warm-water salmon.

So what's a good range of sizes for spinning baits? We can start by taking a leaf out of the fly-fisher's manual. In *Salmon Fishing* Hugh Falkus laid out a rough guide for matching lure size to water temperature: in water from about around 48°F (9°C) to 64°F (18°C), go with lures in the ½ –1½ in (1.5–4 cm) range; in colder water, fish lures in the 2–4 in (5–10 cm) range. Fishing very small baits like this may take a little extra rigging – perhaps involving ledger weights or casting floats (see below) – but it's often worth the effort when the water gets warm. I fish spoons and spinners in the 2–2½ in (5–6 cm) range with fair success once the water gets above about 50°F (10°C), and can still pick up the occasional salmon on still smaller lures in water as warm as 64°F (18°C).

Rough guide to lure size

Water temperature	Lure length
61°F (16°C) +	½ in (1 cm)
56–60°F (14–15°C)	1½–1 in (4–2.5 cm)
51–55°F (11–13°C)	2½–2 in (6–5 cm)
46–50°F (8–10°C)	3½–3 in (9–8 cm)
40–45°F (4–7°C)	6–4 in (15–10 cm)

Going bigger when the water drops below 50°F (10°C) is also worth a shot. After all, mature salmon are used to dealing with big fish both as prey and competitors.[11] At sea they routinely hunt herring, sand eels, capelin, smelts and other bait-fish in the 4–6 in (10–15 cm) range, or even bigger. And the irritating sneaker parr that elicit angry attacks in the river can be that big. Trollers targeting feeding salmon in the sea typically drag big spoons and plugs in the 4–6 in (10–15 cm) range. We'd probably do better on the river if we fished lures a couple of sizes larger, at least when the water is cold.

Lure Flash/Brightness

Another feature to look for in a salmon lure is brightness or flash – by which I mean the way in which it reflects light off its surfaces. This is going to vary depending on what the lure is made of, how it's finished – and, of course, how much light is around to be reflected. Getting this right is mainly a matter of choosing a lure with the correct amount of reflectance – regardless of its colour. Here's where the river angler and the sea angler often part company.

Anglers going after feeding salmon at sea will try to make their lures stand out as much as possible, so a really bright lure is often the first choice. This makes sense when salmon are actually hunting for prey and your lure has to compete for attention with schools of bait-fish. But it usually isn't the best way to get a strike out of salmon in rivers. More effective on the migrating fish is a lure that blends into the river environment, rather than contrasting too strongly with it, yet is still visible once it gets within striking range (see Chapter 3). For salmon in the river we aren't looking for a lure that screams 'Here I come'; we want one that 'sneaks up' on our unsuspecting fish. It's the lure that appears without warning that will trigger a reflex strike.

Bright Day: Bright Lure/Dull Day: Dull Lure

That's the old saying, and it's probably a good rule-of-thumb for the finish on a salmon lure. This is pretty standard stuff among fly-fishers, who typically try to 'match the fly to the water it's swimming in' (see Bailey, p. 41). When Falkus talked about the ideal salmon fly he used words like 'inconspicuous', 'shady', 'tantalizing', 'shadowy' and 'illusory': a lure that's visible but looks natural and blends in (1984, pp. 193–9).

Metallic and mother-of-pearl finishes are especially good choices, because they have what you might call 'self-adjusting flash'. They're highly reflective and flash brightly in good lighting, but they will dim down when the light drops. That's why prey fish typically have silvery reflecting flanks: it allows them to blend into their watery background regardless of light levels. If they keep still, they're hard to see. It's when they flee – or swim irregularly, if hurt or wounded – that their flashing flanks make them a target for any nearby salmon.

There are many anglers who swear by genuine silver-plated spoons and spinners. Silver produces a bright white flash in a range of water conditions, so fish can see it coming at a greater distance than other metal finishes. I've caught many of my fish on real silver, and it is my first choice in a lure aimed at taking feeding salmon as well as sea trout. But I'm beginning to think that nickel, mother-of-pearl, even silver or pearl paint finishes might be better choices for migrating fish. These finishes dim down better when the light decreases, making them more 'illusory' and enhancing the element of surprise.

Metal finishes in descending order of brightness/flash

Polished silver plate (most flash)
Plain chrome
Matte silver and mother-of-pearl
Polished nickel
Polished copper
Gold plate
Polished brass
Polished copper
Dull or tarnished brass
Dull or tarnished copper (least flash)

Cold Water: Bright Lure/Warm Water: Dull Lure

So a lure's relative brightness or flash can be a great attractor. But too much flash can work against you when the water gets warm. Again, it's about metabolism: warm fish, racing metabolism, increased sensitivity to stimuli like bright flashes of light. In warm (clear) water, salmon will avoid a bright lure, so we need to tone it down to be effective. On many rivers the convention is to fish a plain silver or nickel-finish spoon when the water is under 48–50°F (9–10°C) and a plain brass or copper spoon when it's warmer than that. What about all those lures that come finished with less reflective paints? No problem: simply follow the same guidelines: brighter finishes for brighter conditions and cold water, dull lures for duller or lower-light conditions and warm water.

Colour

Some very successful salmon spin-fishers I know choose a lure on the basis of its deliverable action, size and brightness and don't give much more thought to colour. The rest of us like to play the colour game too. So how does colour come into it? First, no one knows for certain whether salmon are attracted to one colour over another. But if you polled anglers, I'm pretty sure red and orange would get the votes for the most likely candidates. Hugh Falkus suggested this might have to do with the fact that male salmon turn reddish when mating: 'The male salmon – like the male stickle-back – turns red in preparation for spawning, presumably to help attract a mate and to ward-off other males' (1984, p. 29). Many well known salmon flies carry at least a little red or orange, and by my count at least half of the commercial spinning baits do too. I usually add a little red or orange to the tails or along the bellies of my own lures, and many other anglers do the same. I don't know if it really matters to the fish, but I figure I've got that base covered if it does.[12]

What is more certain is that salmon, like trout, can detect certain colours better than others, depending on the light and how clear the water is. Like our own, the salmon's eye has rods for detecting colours and cones for detecting shades of grey. But, whereas we do best with greens, salmon do best with blues and reds.[13] In addition, salmon (and sea trout) are able to shift that colour sensitivity, depending on conditions. When feeding at sea their photoreceptors are blue-shifted, like most marine fish. This probably helps them see prey fish in clear blue-green sea waters. But once they've returned to the river, their eyes become more sensitive to colours in the red scale, similar to resident trout. Again, maybe it's related to sexual competition among reddish spawning males.[14]

So red/orange and blue would seem to be good basic colour choices: red/orange generally, and blue when fishing the lower reaches of rivers for newly arrived fish.

Adjusting lure colour for low light

Almost all salmon anglers agree that dawn and dusk are the best times to fish. There are a couple of good reasons for this. One is the typical running pattern of salmon. When the water is more or less clear they tend to migrate from dusk to dawn, and hole up during daylight hours. Running salmon are more aggressive than resting salmon and much more likely to take exception to any creature or object they encounter with a strike. If that happens to be your lure, you might be in for a fight!

The second reason is visibility. Salmon can detect other creatures (and lures) better when the light is low.[15] Like trout, the salmon's eye has a high ratio of rods (light sensitive) to cones (colour sensitive). This means they don't like bright light and can see things better when the light is low, especially around dawn and dusk. On top of that, they can adjust the rods and cones to suit changing conditions. During the day the light-sensitive rods withdraw below the surface of the retina and are shielded by a dark pigment, while the cones extend upward for maximum colour sensitivity. Come dusk, the reverse happens: cones withdraw and rods protrude, giving the salmon maximum sensitivity to contrasts in the grey scale, and so great 'night vision'.[16]

Now, many successful salmon spinners are confident that a salmon will detect their lures regardless of light. They either fish the same lure – say with a metallic finish – round the clock, or they change to a duller lure as the light fades. But many others try to get the extra edge by using lure colours that fish can detect a little more easily once the sun has set, or when it's very cloudy or overcast.

It is a fact that some colours are more visible under diminished light conditions than others. To sum up some pretty daunting physics, long-wavelength colours fade and black out more quickly than short-wavelength colours as light diminishes. This is the order: red goes first, then orange, yellow, green and blue. So red is the least visible under low light conditions, say from dusk to dawn, and blue the most visible. Black is also visible when viewed against a lighter background. So black, blue and white, alone or in combination, are age-old colour choices for fishing for salmon in low light. Today, many anglers also use lures with fluorescent and glow-paint finishes. Both are highly visible under low-light conditions but I've found they work best when used sparingly. Too much, and a lure can stand out like a sore thumb and lose its subtle appeal.[17]

Adjusting lure colour for turbid water

That's for clear water. What about when the water has got some colour in it – what the experts call turbid water? No problem. In fact, a little colour in the water actually helps our chances. Salmon feel more secure in coloured water, and so are significantly more likely to smash a lure than in water that's dead clear, where they feel more exposed.[18]

The experts don't all agree on how much turbidity is ideal for spinning. Pacific Coast anglers after steelhead (rainbow) trout say green water means 'go' and 3–3½ ft (90–110 cm) of visibility is considered perfect. Sea-trout fishers look for slightly off-coloured water too – the traditional 'pale lager beer or very weak coffee' conditions. In my experience, clarity with anywhere from about 3–6 ft (90–180 cm) of visibility fishes best for salmon.

It is harder for salmon to detect our offerings when the water is less than clear. So in turbid water we need to make our lures a bit more visible. One way is simply by going to a bigger lure. This is a good move when the water is cold and we don't need to worry about spooking fish as much. But a better solution, which works at any temperature, is to add some colours. Not the same colours we use for low light. What we want now are the long-wavelength colours like red, orange, yellow and chartreuse (yellow-green). These are the colours that suspended particles in the water (turbidity) scatter or diffuse more slowly than short-wavelength colours like purple, blue and green. So they'll remain the most visible to fish when the water is less than clear. Fluorescent shades of red, orange, yellow and green are also highly visible in coloured water, as are black-and-white patterns.

How about when the water is turbid *and* the light poor? These are tough conditions. But, if you're up for the challenge, try fishing your biggest lure with a high-contrast pattern; try fluorescents, glow-paint, and black/blue-and-white combinations. There is no room for subtlety in these conditions – you want a lure that screams! Good luck.

Pattern

The way colour appears on a lure is called pattern. The bait-fisher has essentially two options. One is to fish the lure with a single-colour finish – whether natural metal or some applied finish – usually called a monochrome pattern. Spoons and spinners in natural metallic finishes are essentially monochrome patterns; so are plugs or minnows painted in tints or shades of a single colour, metallic or otherwise. The other choice is lures with multiple colours – polychrome patterns. Both schemes rely on making the lure visible to the fish by means of contrast. Monochrome patterns mainly control how much the lure stands out against the background, while polychrome patterns rely more on internal contrasts to attract attention.

Nobody can tell you which makes the most effective salmon lure – if there is one. The better salmon spinners I know favour monochrome or very simple two-colour patterns, and when asked they nearly all say pattern doesn't really matter as much as action, size and brightness. There are others, though, who swear by certain – sometimes intricate – polychrome patterns.

Many salmon spinners nowadays fish lifelike fish patterns,

some by choice but most (I'd guess) because many lures come off the shelf that way, and people don't bother changing them. Natural fish patterns are probably as good as any when fishing clear water. Like plain metallic finishes, they tend to blend in and look natural. But when it comes to turbid water, simple geometric patterns are a better choice.

There is a growing body of research on fish vision confirming what old-time spinning anglers have known all along: that salmon and trout respond best to simple geometric shapes (see Wallbridge, and Taylor). Before the modern proliferation of super-realistic fish patterns, most of the popular salmon lures carried simple geometric shapes featuring stripes, bars, dots, diagonals and diamonds. Remember the Five of Diamonds, the Dardevle (candycane), the zebra, the tiger, the Blair (with its raised pimple-dots)? They worked when they were new, and they work now. When the water goes dirty I usually turn to an orange tiger pattern – fluorescent orange with black stripes – simple and visible.

Unfortunately, lures with simple geometric patterns aren't always so easy to find. So, when I can't find what I want, I scrape off the stock finish and apply my own patterns, using paint, a marker pen or tape. Remember, salmon (like trout) are pretty near-sighted, and turbid water only makes it harder for them to detect our lures. A highly visible geometric pattern can mean the difference between a lure passing by unnoticed and getting slammed!

Sound and Smell

Salmon, like trout, are primarily what biologists call visual predators. Whether or not another creature – or our lure – elicits a strike mainly rests on how it looks or moves. So action and appearance should be main considerations when choosing lures. But fish also use other senses to detect and pursue prey, competitors or lures. Hearing is one. Salmon do have internal 'ears', but they 'hear' primarily by picking up vibrations via the thin, dark lateral line running down each flank. All lures displace water, and so send out sound waves, which fish 'hear' via this line. The sense of smell is also well developed. After all, that's mainly how salmon navigate back to their native spawning rivers from hundreds of miles away at sea. So a lure that can also be detected by smell – at least if it's an attractive smell – will be more effective than one that can't (or that smells bad). Obviously, the best lures will incorporate all the sensory stimuli: visual, auditory and olfactory.

Choosing Lures

Different spin-baits tend to become popular on different rivers. On some the spoon rules among bank anglers. For boaters it's the diving plug. In other areas it might be the Flying C or the Devon.

Why do certain lures become popular on certain rivers and not others? Some believe it's a particular taste preference among local fish. Could be. But more likely it's about lure control. It's simply easier to deliver some lures to the right depth with the right speed and action on some stretches of water than others. Once anglers hit on these lures, their presentations improve, better catches follow and other spin-baits fade in popularity. That's why a good first move before you start buying (or making) lures is to ask what the local old-timers use. Those will be the lures that generations of anglers through trial and error have found perform best on that particular water. I always start with them; then experiment with others. So whether you end up fishing mostly spoons, spinners, plugs or other types of spin-baits is going to depend mainly on the kind of water you generally fish and also how you fish it. Here's the low-down on the different types of spin-lures available, along with their strengths and weaknesses.

Spoons

Nobody knows who first got the idea that a salmon might be attracted to a spoon-shaped lure. It might have been the reputed inventor of the spoon-bait in England, whom Henry Cholmondeley-Pennell tells of meeting in his *The Book of the Pike* (1865). He described the lure: 'It is simply a bowl of a good-sized plated spoon, with two large Pike hooks soldered roughly on to the inside of the small end' (p. 226). He also included an etching of a similar early spoon which I've reproduced here. That additional flying outrigger hook is rare today, although some modern Finnish spoons like the Kuusamo Professor still carry them.

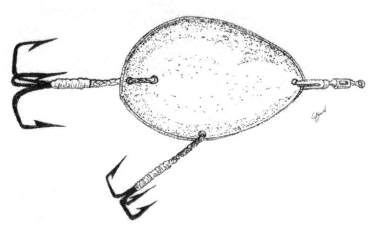

Early spoons were made by sawing the bowl off a soup spoon and attaching a swivel and some hooks, and were usually intended for taking pike. This one, from Cholmondeley-Pennell's *The Book of the Pike* (1865), has a flying outrigger treble.

As for how it was discovered, Cholmondeley-Pennell's inventor related what was becoming, it seems, the canonical story of a spoon that was mistakenly dropped overboard and taken by a fish. In his version it was a pike in the River Exe that grabbed it as it 'went wavering down through the water' (p. 226). Notably, America's spoon inventor Julio T. Buel told the same story, only the fish was a trout, and the water a lake in Vermont (H. Thompson, *The Spooners*). More importantly, Cholmondeley-Pennell went on to say (p. 227):

> I, in common with probably most other spinners, took strongly to the Spoon-bait when it first became generally known in this country . . . Its advantage over most other artificial baits is that

it is as killing with Trout, both sea and freshwater, and also with the Perch, as with the Pike, *and even the lordly Salmon is not altogether insensible to its attractions.*

In any event, many anglers today consider the spoon their 'bread-and-butter' salmon lure, myself included. The main reasons are control and versatility. It's simply easier to put a spoon where it needs to be under a wider range of water conditions than it is with other lures. You can fish spoons high and low, fast or slow, in heavy water and light. They are also very effective!

Spoon Action

Different spoons can look very different when they are moving through water. This is the result of some pretty complex hydrodynamics. But put simply: a spoon's *action* results from the opposing water pressures on the spoon body's irregular surfaces, in conjunction with the opposing drag set up by the tail hook.

Remember, a spoon lure has essentially two working parts: the spoon body and the tail hook. They work together to achieve the spoon's characteristic fish-attracting action. So how a spoon looks in the water is going to depend on a number of things: the overall shape, weight and size of the spoon body, along with the weight, size and type of hook and how it's attached (one or two split rings for example), as well as how fast the spoon is travelling against the current.

Now, many spoon-fishers will tell you they take salmon and sea trout on the same spoons. Fishing the same spoons for both is common on the waters I fish. That's OK. But the more experienced salmon spinners choose their spoons with the target fish in mind. They'll tell you that trout and salmon 'prefer' different kinds of actions in a spoon. For trout, it's one with a highly irregular, darting action. This will attract hits from salmon too, but a spoon that keeps a more regular, rhythmic action – something like a steady, throbbing wobble – will get you more strikes from salmon. Can I be more specific? Let's say a spoon that keeps a steady rhythm of 3–6 beats per second.

In fact, what seems to separate the really successful salmon spoon-fishers from the rest is their ability to keep their spoon fishing at the right frequency in all kinds of water – fast, slow, shallow, deep, etc. Spoon mastery comes in *keeping the beat*. Since a spoon's action depends on a number of variables, getting really proficient means knowing how spoons of different shapes, sizes and weights perform at different speeds in different types of flow, and knowing when you need to change from one to another to keep the right action going. Most spoon-fishers watch the tip of their rod to keep an eye on their spoon's movements. Or, if they're using very sensitive superbraid line, they feel the spoon body tossing itself from side-to-side rhythmically through their hands. When it's throbbing at around 3–6 beats per second, you know you're fishing!

Types of Spoon

Learning how to keep the beat will come only from plenty of experience of fishing different flows. But here's a useful approach that's worked for me. It's a system for keeping your spoon fishing with the right action by switching between designs and weights.[19] The system calls for four spoon designs (fat, skinny, thin-blade and jigging).

Fat or Wide-body Spoons

These are spoons with wider profiles.[20] In plan view the shape can be a fat teardrop, oval, football, or so-called classic (where the widest point is near the base or tail). In section, the curvature is usually a gentle 'S', 'C' or 'J' shape. The wider bodies make these spoons more buoyant than narrower, elongated spoons. Fat spoons are a good choice for keeping the beat in moderate flows and mid-pool drifts down to say 15 ft (4.5 m) deep, or in very shallow runs, along slacker edge water when the river is running high, or when you are drifting it with the current. Many companies produce good wide-body models suited for salmon (see box). One, the Blair Spoon, has been the standard on British rivers for who knows how long. According to Hugh Falkus it was created by ex-ghillie turned tackle-dealer William Blair of Kincardine O'Neil on the Aberdeen-shire River Dee (1984, p. 332). It's got the unique feature of bumps all along the convex side, which cause extra turbulence and, many feel, make the spoon more detectable and attractive to salmon. Blairs are getting harder to find, though. But try:

D & E Hughes Fishing Tackle, 24 Penlan Street, Pwllheli, Gwynedd, LL53 5DE
Turriff Tackle & Trophies, 6 Castle Street, Turriff, Aberdeen-shire, AB53 4BJ

Some good wide-body spoon choices

Abu's Salar and Plankton (used only), Hammer, Sländan, Lill'Öring, Atom, Utö and Flamingo (Abu Garcia)

Acme's Little Cleo, Stee-Lee, Wob-L-Rite, KO Wobbler (Acme Tackle, Inc.)

Blue Fox's Quiver, Inkoo and Esox/Flash (Blue Fox)

Blair Spoon (various companies make one)

Cabela's Canadian and Diamond spoons (Cabela's)

Dick Nite's Spoon (Dick Nite)

Eppinger's Devle Dog and Red Eye (Eppinger Mfg. Co)

Fishing Pool's Atlantic and Whitewater spoons (Fishing Pool)

Gibbs Koho and Kit-A-Mat (Gibbs/Nortac)

Hansen's Thor, Flash (Hansen)

J.R. Tackle's Carlson Salmon Spoons (J.R. Tackle Co.)

Johnson's Silver Minnow Sprite (Johnson Co.)

Kuusamo's Professor, Räsänen (Kuusamo)

Luhr Jensen's Krocodile Stubby, Tony Accetta's Spoon (Luhr Jensen and Sons, Inc.)

Pen-Tac's BC Steel (Pen-Tac Inc.)

Wiggler's Iron Wiggler (Wiggler)

Williams Whitefish and Wabler (Williams)

Worden's Wonder Lure and Wob-lure (Worden's Lures/Yakima Bait Co.)

Skinny or Elongated Spoons

These spoons have long, thin profiles with a fairly radical 'S' curvature (foil) along the axis.[21] They are much less buoyant than fat spoons, so they sink faster and only wobble at higher water velocities. Skinny spoons are a good first choice when working across or against deep, strong flows, or in very fast currents. In lighter weights these spoons are also ideal for high, fast presentations.

Of the pack, the Toby has long been a first choice on many waters. The original is made by Abu Garcia. But many companies now make cheaper lookalikes that seem to work just as well (see box). These spoons probably account for more salmon than all the other spoons combined, at least on European rivers. But Tobies and similar spoons have one legendary drawback: poor hook-ups and lost fish! Chronic sufferers have come up with a variety of fixes to improve the hooking efficiency of these otherwise excellent spoons.[22] Hugh Falkus improved his Tobies by preventing the treble from flying about by 'stiffening the link with tape', and reconnecting the treble via a 'flying mount' (1984, p. 422). I've come up with my own version of a flying mount for all my longer skinny spoons (see box).

Connecting the treble via two split rings also seems to improve hook-ups, and Abu now sells its larger Toby models this way. Some anglers, like those on the River Tay, find that filing off the Toby's rear fins also improves hooking efficiency.

Flying mount for skinny spoons

If you are losing too many hooked fish, try this: Remove the split rings fore and aft of the suspect spoon. Leave the treble attached to one. Now take two short pieces of thin wire (steel or copper baling wire or stripped electrical wire about 1mm in diameter will do). Fold each piece in two and push these through the holes in the spoon body to make two loops or eyes protruding from the spoon's concave face. Bend the tails of

---

each wire flat against the convex face to hold them in place (I find it easier to do this if I insert a nail through each eye).

To rig this up for fishing simply thread your monofilament leader through both eyes and tie it directly to the split ring with the treble. When a salmon takes hold the spoon body slides up the leader, affording the fish no leverage and leaving it to fight the treble alone.

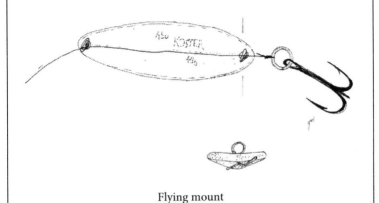

Flying mount

Some good skinny spoon choices

Abu's Toby, Toby Salmo, and Toby Rocket (Abu Garcia)
Blue Fox's Inkoo Vivid and Moresilda (Blue Fox)
Eppinger's Cop-E-Cat (Eppinger Mfg. Co)
Fläden's Öring (Fläden)
Hansen's Pilgrim, Fight (Hansen of Denmark)

Luhr Jensen's Coyote, Krocodile and Needlefish (Luhr Jensen Co.)
Mepps' Syclops (Mepps)
Ron Thompson's Slimline (Ron Thompson)
Viking's Herring (Viking)

Dampening a spoon's action

Some elongated spoons tend to produce very erratic darting actions at higher speeds – great for sea trout, not for salmon. To get these spoons fishing with a more rhythmic, wobbling action, try fishing them in heavier models more slowly. Or try doubling the spoon's density by 'sandwiching' two identical spoon bodies together on one set of split rings. An added bonus is that a sandwich-spoon will rattle while it wobbles, and that can only make it more attractive as a target. Paul Fishlock of Perthshire tells me this is a common trick among River Tay anglers. You can also dampen a spoon's action by adding a bead or some yarn to the hook shaft, or by attaching a swivel or snap swivel directly to the spoon's front eye.

Thin-blade Spoons

There will be times when you want to work a spoon along the bottom very, very slowly: as when the water is icy cold or very turbid. Or you might want to hang it in a slow current behind an anchored boat (see Chapter 3). Regular casting spoons are usually too heavy to slow down enough without hanging them up on the bottom. What you want for this kind of fishing is a more buoyant thin-blade spoon. These are sometimes called trolling spoons, flutter spoons, or wobles, and a good number of companies make them. Most are designed for trolling still waters, but they can often be used to fish currents too. Northern King models NKC5, NK4D and NK28 have served me well for salmon as well as sea trout. But those made by other companies – like Ismo, Diamond King, Pure-lure or Break Point – are also worth a try.

It will probably take some trial and error before you find a thin-blade spoon that keeps the desired action in the currents you'll be fishing. Start with the smaller models weighing around ½ oz (13–15 g), measuring 2½ to 3½ in (4–10 cm) and designed to perform at speeds between 1½ and 3½ mph (2.5 and 5.5 kmph). I've tried the big 'magnum' models too, but find they are simply too hard to cast accurately or control in heavy water. Nowadays, I tend to make all my own thin-blades (see Appendix).

Jigging Spoons

Jigging spoons have long been a favourite of mine for sea trout. More and more I find I'm fishing them for salmon too, because they work! Jigging spoons are built differently from other spoons. They're usually straight, thick, compact slabs of metal somewhere between rectangular and biconvex in shape. They don't have much action on a steady retrieve but they do sink fast, so you can move them vertically through the water with a nice controlled sink-and-draw (jigging) motion. It's usually on the drop that a salmon will take a jigging spoon, so the very best have a seductive wiggle action when they sink. Plenty of companies make spoons suited to jigging. I make all my own, and it's easy as pie (see Appendix).

Good choices for jigging spoons

Swedish Pimple (Bay de Noc)	Krill (Abu Garcia)
Nils Master Jig (Nils Master)	Fazet, Phantom and
Crippled Herring (Luhr	Solvpilen (Ron
Jensen)	Thompson)
Kastmaster (Acme)	Pilken and Tobis (Jensen)

Reversing a spoon's direction

Many skinny spoons work well as jigging spoons if you run them in the opposite direction. Simply slip the treble off the tail ring, slide it onto the head ring and fish it 'backwards'. It might not look so appealing on the draw, but it may wiggle nicely on the drop. Try it!

Spinners

Most salmon anglers today use essentially two kinds of spinners, conventional blade spinners, sometimes called simply 'blades' (which include the Mepps, Flying C and similar lures) and artificial minnows, more commonly called just 'minnows', including the Devon and its local variants. Although design details can vary, these lures all rely on the flickering light reflections and sound vibrations sent off by the lure's whirling action to attract fish. A spinner's vibrations make it especially effective in coloured water, since fish can detect it coming via their lateral lines even before it gets into visual range.

Blade Spinners

Blade spinners have changed very little since they first appeared in the mid-nineteenth century. Then, as now, these lures featured one or more blades that rotate around a central axis. Most have a central steel wire shaft mounted with several metal or plastic beads or cylinders for friction and weight, and a single (sometimes tandem) steel blade attached by a clevis (or set of swivels) so it spins when you pull it through the water, along with a hook, usually a treble.

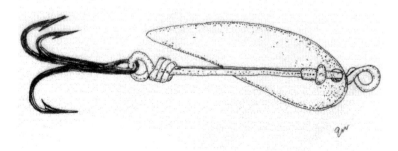

This nineteenth-century blade spinner looks much
like those used today.

Mepps and Others

The best known of the modern blade spinners is probably the Mepps. This French-made lure has been around for many years and probably accounts for more salmon and sea trout than any other single spinner. Like spoons, Mepps come in a range of sizes and finishes. Sizes are usually numbered from tiny No. 00's to large No. 7s, with the normal salmon range running from 3 to 5 and weighing ¼–½ oz (7–14 g). Mepps used to publish a useful guide for choosing among their models (see box below).

Mepps guide to spinner selection

For cold (50°F (10°C) or less) clear water:
Cloudy conditions: No. 5 spinner with silver blade and pink decal with green dots
Sunny conditions: No. 5 spinner with silver blade and green decal with pink dots
Low-light/shade conditions: No. 5 spinner with silver blade and black decal with glow dots

For cold (50°F (10°C) or less) turbid-muddy water:
No. 5 spinner with gold blade and black decal with fluorescent chartreuse dots

For cool (51–59°F (10.5–15°C)) clear water:
Cloudy conditions: No. 4 spinner with gold blade and black decal with green dots
Sunny conditions: No. 4 spinner with black blade and fluorescent chartreuse decal with black dots
Low-light/shade conditions: No. 4 spinner with silver blade and black decal with glow dots

---

For cool (51–59°F (10.5–15°C)) turbid-muddy water:
No. 5 spinner with gold blade and black decal with fluorescent chartreuse dots

For warm (60°F (15.5°C) plus) clear water:
Cloudy conditions: No. 3 spinner with tarnished brass blade and green decal with black dots
Sunny conditions: No. 3 spinner with coffee blade
Low-light/shade conditions: No. 3 spinner with silver blade and black decal with glow dots

For warm (60°F (15.5°C) plus) turbid-muddy water:
No. 4 spinner with gold blade and black decal with fluorescent chartreuse dots

Many companies make high quality blade spinners suited to salmon. The single-blade spinner is most common. But companies like Hildebrandt and EGB also make tandem models. The shape of the blade is critical: oval and round-bladed models like Mepps Aglia, Blue Fox Vibrax or Abu Droppen are best for slower flows and speeds, or for fishing with the current. Longer-bladed models like Mepps Aglia Long, and Blue Fox Deep Super Vibrax and Salmon Super Vibrax are better for faster retrieves and stronger currents. Silver, copper and gold are the standard finishes. Some manufacturers like Mepps, Hildebrandt and the Swiss EGB plate their blades with real silver or gold. Colour patterns, if any, come on the outside of the blade, sometimes on the shaft.

The trick of being effective with these lures lies in choosing the right combinations of size and shape, so the blade revolves at the right frequency, regardless of the water. Remember, a slow action is what you want in a salmon lure –we aren't looking for a spinner that takes off into the current buzzing like a motor! You want one with a blade that kicks over at a low frequency, producing a steady, rhythmic thrumming. It won't be as visible on the rod tip, or as detectable in the fingers, as a spoon – at least not at first. But after some time you'll learn to see and feel the difference between a spinner that's gone dead, one that's racing too fast, and one that's keeping the right beat. Most anglers carry several different spinners and change them as needed, others replace the stock clevis with a quick-change clevis and carry a bunch of different blades instead. Fishing Pool Ltd in Coventry carries both (www.fishingpool.co.uk).

Many salmon and sea trout anglers swear by blade spinners for high, fast retrieves with the current (see 'Upstreaming' in Chapter 3) because the light blade revolves (and attracts) even against low water resistance. Some say they are also less likely to spook keyed-up warm-water fish. But for working across or against the current, especially on deep presentations, spinners aren't always the best choice. Reason: lack of control. Once the blade 'catches' the water and starts spinning, the lure tends to 'take on a mind of its own'. Both the spinner's direction and depth can be hard to control, especially in fast water.

Flying Cs

On British waters the Flying C spinner ranks right next to Mepps in popularity for salmon and sea trout. It's built similarly to other spinners but is usually bigger and heavier, and it has a signature feature – a long rubber sheath frayed at the end: the 'condom' or 'C' part of the lure. The C covers a long body made of steel, lead, plastic or sometimes balsa wood.

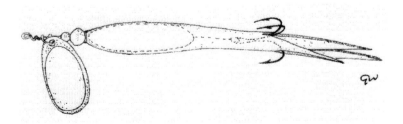

The Flying C spinner is one of the most popular lures for salmon on British waters.

Some say one of the keys to the C's effectiveness, besides the flickering blade, is that rubber sheath, which they feel enhances vibrations. A treble hook (sometimes a single) and one or two oval spinner blades up at the head complete the package. The C seems to be an Irish invention, but now they are widely available from companies like Fishing Pool, Ron Thompson, even Mepps. Where Mepps-type spinners work best in lighter flows, the C is usually the better choice for heavy water, with sizes 3 (⅜ oz/10.5 g), 4 (⅝ oz/17.5 g) and 5 (⅞ oz/24.75 g) the most common. Like many of the larger spinners it's often necessary to 'kick-start' the C's blade into action by giving a quick snap of the wrist once it's in the water.

Flying Cs are normally fished flatline – that is, with no additional weight. This is effective, but over snaggy bottoms hang-ups can be more the rule than the exception. So some anglers have started making floating models and fishing these off ledger rigs to cut down on snags. A few companies have picked up on this and started making them too; one is Fishing Pool Ltd. Flying Cs can be found in a range of finishes. Popular 'condom' colours are yellow, black, silver or purple, with blades in silver or copper, or painted.

Minnows

On many salmon rivers, minnows see as much water time as Tobies, Mepps and Cs. Minnows are also spinners, but built differently. The body is a hollow cigar-shaped shell with a couple of fins, so it rotates around an axis (the wire or monofilament trace, or 'flight') attached to a trailing treble hook. Artificial minnows probably haven't been around as long as wobbling lures like spoons. But they do go back a few centuries at least. Izaak Walton in the 1676 edition of his much celebrated book *The Compleat Angler* (p. 99) gave detailed directions for making them, as did many later authors. However, as noted above, these early spinners were considered mainly trout and pike lures until the later nineteenth century, when bait-anglers realized they worked just as well on salmon.

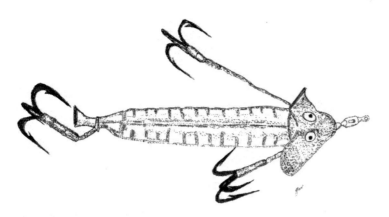

The Phantom minnow first appeared in the mid-nineteenth century
and, alongside the Devon, became one of the first spinning baits used
in harling for salmon. It commonly had a natural skin or silk body
and carried up to four flying trebles.

The earliest minnow seems to have evolved from a favourite pike
and trout lure – the natural dead-bait. These were whole dead
minnows skewered on a long pin (the trace, or flight) with one or
more hooks, and arranged so that they would spin when drawn
through the water. At some point – probably in the early nineteenth
century – a simple propeller called the pectoral fin was added to
some flights up at the head to promote more reliable spinning. Over
time, the dead fish was replaced by an artificial look-alike, fashioned
from materials like lead, tin, polished iron, silver, ivory, wood, cork,
mother-of-pearl, sewn fabrics, quill, carp scale, whale bone, even
real fish skin. Some were painted to look more or less realistic. By the
end of the century, minnows looked much the way they do today.
The original Phantoms and Devons were some of the first artificial
spin-baits to be fished – alongside flies – off the backs of harling
boats on rivers like the Tay and Shannon (see Francis, p. 9, and
Black). The Devon remains the most popular minnow for salmon.
But there are numerous local versions including the more slender
'Bull-nosed', the fat-bodied 'Severn', the lighter hazel-wood 'Wye',
and the flat-sided 'Sprat' that gives off a bit more flash than most.
    Some minnows are made of heavy metal, even lead, so you can
fish them flatline. But most experienced minnow spinners fish

buoyant wood or plastic models off ledger rigs using either in-line or dropper weights. This way they can keep them swimming tight along a snaggy bottom as slowly as they want – even motionless in the current – with fewer hang-ups. For minnows, like other spinning baits, are most effective when they spin *slowly*. They don't have much flash. But if they're painted in the standard two-tone colour scheme – one down the back and one along the belly – they do give off a low frequency blink. This, along with its subtle wiggle, makes it a lure salmon just love to slam!

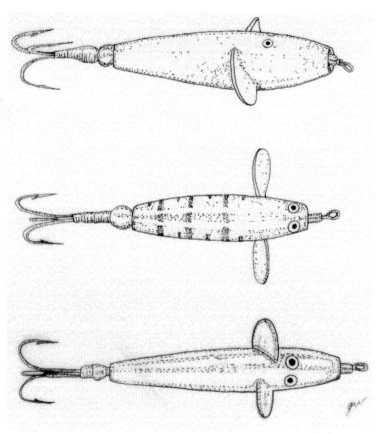

Minnows have become a staple on many salmon rivers in Britain. Among the numerous local varieties are here pictured the Severn (top), Wye (middle), and traditional Devon (bottom).

One of the advantages of minnows over other spin baits is their great hooking and holding qualities. They don't have much lateral action, so fish can grab the tail (hook) more cleanly. They're also nearly impossible for a hooked fish to lever off. Once a fish is on and starts to roll, the shell body slides up the leader, and the hooked fish is left to fight the treble alone.

Minnows come in just about any colour you want, but the most popular seem to be green and yellow (commonly known as the yellow-belly), brown and gold, black and gold, and (when the water get very cold and clear) blue and silver. Sizes range from about 3 in (7.5 cm) for cold water down to about 1 in (2.5 cm) for warm water.

If you are fishing in Britain you can find Devons and other minnows in almost any tackle shop. If you're fishing foreign waters you'll want to pack some along, or turn to one of the big British mail-order houses like Fishing Pool Ltd (www.fishingpool.co.uk), The Devon Minnow Store (www.thedevonminnowstore.co.uk) or John Norris of Penrith (www.johnnorris.co.uk). Alternatively, you can make them yourself (see Appendix).

Diving Plugs

If you get serious about harling for salmon you'll need a few diving plugs. Like Devons, these are buoyant or semi-buoyant lures with fat, plug-shaped bodies. The difference is that these have a bevel, bill or lip at the front, so they dive down when being pulled through the water. Fished flatline they will dive anywhere from 2–18 ft (0.5–5.5 m).

One of the advantages of diving plugs is their buoyancy. Like Devons, they can be fished deep with dropper weights over a snaggy bottom without the hang-ups you would suffer with spoons or spinners. So they're perfect for trolling or hanging in a current off the back of an anchored boat. Another plus is their action. Fished fast, these plugs dart and wiggle frantically, which makes them excellent for sea trout. But they can also be fished much slower – right down to a near stop – to get just the kind of laboured wobbling action salmon go for.

Getting the action right takes experience, though: diving plugs' actions respond in different ways to changes in water resistance. Some models keep a nice laboured wobble only in slower currents; others move well in faster water. Which models will work best for you will depend on the kind of water you fish. Finding out what local experts use is a good way to narrow down the field. Generally speaking, the wider the diving lip, bevel or bill, the slower the water resistance (or lure speed) needed to attain a nice, slow wiggle. Try several until you find those that keep the right action in the kinds of current you normally fish.

Sound is another feature. Most diving plugs nowadays are made with internal balls that rattle and send out vibrations which help salmon find them, especially in turbid water and low light. Plugs also hook and hold fish well. Most are hung with at least two trebles, sometimes three. No matter where a salmon grabs a plug, it usually ends up with at least one hook in its mouth. Even an initially poor hook-up often improves when other hooks on the plug take hold during the fight. But do check whether there are single-hook restrictions in force which require you to remove one or two – the belly hook, preferably (see box below).

Rapalas

Originally, plugs were all made of balsa wood or cork; now most are moulded plastic. One of the few makers that still offers balsa wood is Rapala. These plugs are popular almost everywhere you find salmon (and sea trout) spinners. The original floating balsa-wood model created in Finland by Lainu Rapala in the 1940s is still a first choice for many. Where I fish, the Rapala original jointed model (2½ in/6.5 cm) is a favourite for both salmon and sea trout. Common colour choices are silver and blue for colder water, and gold and red for warmer water. Other popular Rapalas are the X-Rap, Husky Jerk, Magnum and Team Esko – all floating – along with the slow-sinking Countdown.

Other Plugs

Besides Rapala, what's popular depends mostly on where you fish. On my home waters, it's the Nils Master Spearhead in orange and black, Coton Cordell's Ripplin' Red Fin in metallic blue or gold (or repainted in orange) along with various plugs by Strike Pro, and Bomber. On other waters, Rapalas are joined by the Kynock Killer (a British variant of the Canadian J-plug) or near copies like the ACE Minnow by Fishing Pool. A Scottish plug called the Tadpole (made by Salmo, and best described as a Devon with a Flying C-type 'condom') is getting popular on some rivers; you can find it at www.tacklebargains.co.uk. So is the Canadian Wiggler – a hollow-brass, flatfish-type plug made by Lindquist Bros Bait Co. Ltd in Ontario. Most of these plugs come in a range of sizes, but those most widely used for river salmon range from about 2½–7 in (6.5–18 cm) long.

How about casting diving plugs? Theoretically, yes. Almost all these plugs can be had in sinking models heavy enough to cast from shore. But I don't know many fishers who do this. After trying it myself I know why: once a heavy diving plug starts digging itself down into the current, it's even harder to control than a big spinner. If you want to cast them, try one of the floating models. Fish it flat-line with an in-line lead or dropper weight rigging to help get it out and down.

Snag-proofing diving plugs

If you are snagging the bottom a lot with your Rapala-like diving plugs, try this:

Remove the belly treble (that's the one that usually snags) and replace it with a short piece of bailing wire. You will still hook enough fish, but you'll snag the bottom less often and also save hooks! On rivers where there is a one-treble-per-lure rule you're required to do this anyway (see 'Know the regulations' box, p. 136).

Many plugs can be tuned at the waterside, and often need to be. If the plug is diving to the left, try turning the front screw eye (where you tie the leader) clockwise or bending it left. If it's diving to the right, turn the screw eye anticlockwise, or bend it to the right. Unfortunately, Kynock Killer/J-plug types, where the line or trace runs through the body, aren't tunable, except for reshaping the front bevel with a file (see Appendix).

A warning: diving plugs are hi-tech lures with narrow design tolerances. That means only the best of them – the brand names – will work reliably, and those are going to cost perhaps two to three times the price of a spoon or spinner. But if you're looking for a challenge, and a way to save money, you can try making your own (see Appendix).

How About Smell?

Many waters prohibit the use of natural or artificial baits or scents. Where it is allowed, some bait-fishers add these to their normal hardware offerings – a move that's sometimes called *tipping*. Tipping can make a good lure even better. Even though most salmon aren't interested in feeding once they are in the river, it's no surprise that a lure that smells more like the real thing – or at least doesn't smell like something alarming – is going to attract more strikes. And, from what I've heard from experienced tippers, they do. We know that salmon have a highly developed sense of smell. They use it for homing in on their spawning streams and, along with sight and 'hearing', to detect prey, competitors and potential predators, like bears and humans. So tipping not only enhances a lure's attractiveness, it also masks odours that might turn fish away.

Bait Tails

Maybe the most popular tipping method is to hang some cut bait off the treble hook of a spoon or spinner. Strips of herring, squid, sometimes scented PowerBait worms, are pretty common. It's simple and, according to users, effective. It's also a good way to tame a spoon's over-wild action. But you need to keep a close eye on any lure that's carrying bait to make sure it still moves the way you want it to.

Commercial Smears and Oils

You don't have to deal with cut bait to get the benefits of a good-smelling lure. The alternative is to use scents you smear on. By now almost everybody has heard of PowerBait – that smelly, pasty dough made by the Berkley company. It's usually advertised as a trout bait, but salmon seem to like it too. Not surprising, since it smells something like old shrimp. Nowadays many other companies make scents for fishing as well; some even specifically for salmon and steelhead trout. Mike's Lunker Lotion, Smelly Jelly, Pro-Cure Anise Plus and Sandshrimp have earned good reputations among salmon anglers on the Pacific Coast. A few companies are also experimenting with pheromone-based scents like Rapala's Ultrabite. These contain certain amino acids that work as a sexual attractant.

But you don't have to buy scents. Some anglers mix their own special concoctions. According to the pros at Fish Sponge, basic ingredients include fish oils like cod's liver, tuna, herring, sardine, etc., or oils rich in omega-3 amino acids like canola (rapeseed) oil, along with sugar, salt, molasses and some spices – especially anise, which salmon apparently really like. Devotees smear this stuff on their lures, lines, even hands, and swear that it translates to more salmon on the hook. Seems worth a try, if you don't mind the mess.

Covering Bad Odours

If salmon can detect a good-smelling lure, they can detect a bad-smelling one too. What's bad? Well, we know a few things that seem to repel salmonids. One is humans. We've long known that salmon react negatively to even small traces of human odour in the water. Apparently the culprit is an amino acid called serine which is found in the human skin (see Idler *et al*). So rinsing your hands off upstream of targeted lies is a definite no-no. Other potential turn-offs include sunscreen lotions, insect repellent, certain cosmetic fragrances, nicotine from tobacco, and the alcohol you find in those little packaged waterless wipes.

Covering up smells that might turn a fish away is another reason to consider tipping your lures with bait or smearing your hands and tackle with scent. But there is another way too – spraying your hands or lures or both with a light petroleum oil. It might not attract salmon, but it seems to mask bad odours. WD-40 has long been the angler's standard. At the very least, keep your hands clean of the turn-off smells when handling tackle. And if you're going to be wading, watch out for contaminants on your boots too.

I don't normally tip my lures. For me, the mess and extra hassle are rarely worth it: I catch enough on straight hardware. But I know plenty of successful hardware users who do tip, and on some Pacific Coast rivers it's standard practice. I will confess to sometimes carrying a bottle of fluorescent orange PowerBait dough in the bottom of my tackle bag. And there are times when it comes in handy, say, to smell-up a lure being used in turbid water, or to cover up suspect contaminants on my hands.

Hooks

The most important piece of tackle is the hook. It's the tail of your lure, which is what a salmon usually targets. A broken hook, a bent or dull hook, a too small or too large hook, a weak hook or a hook that a striking fish can't get hold of – all can mean a lost chance.

That may seem blindingly obvious. But you would be surprised how many anglers overlook hook quality. For sea trout, you can sometimes get away with mediocre hooks. But not for salmon. Salmon are bigger, stronger and have much harder mouths. They're also prone to nasty (and exciting) habits like savage head-shaking, repeated jumping, quick U-turns, and hell-for-leather runs towards the sea. Any salmon worth its name can render a poor quality hook unrecognizable in less than a couple of minutes, and nearly always very empty! I learnt this the hard way, trying to save a few shillings with cheap hooks. To take a salmon you need a hook that's sharp and strong enough to penetrate its tough bony mouth and not bend during the fight.

Single or treble? In the past few years it's become fashionable, especially in North America, to replace trebles with single hooks on many spinning baits. Converts say they hold onto hooked fish better. I've fished them both to check this out, and have to concede that a fish well hooked on a single tends to stay there. Singles bite deeper than trebles and are harder for a fighting fish to lever loose. I also know from experience that singles miss many hook-ups that trebles wouldn't. There were times I felt my single-hook lure being slammed or tugged by a salmon with impunity. No surprise here: it's a simple matter of three hooks versus one.

Single hooks may be OK when you're fishing for salmon at sea. These are hunting fish, which we know from film recordings may repeatedly strike the same lure until they latch on. But most river salmon aren't bent on eating our lures, only on damaging them or chasing them away. The attacks are less direct – slashing bites and tail snaps – and less persistent. It stands to reason that a lure with three-way hooking coverage will grab more fish than a lure with one-way coverage. This isn't just my opinion. Many guides recommend their clients bring their lures rigged with trebles.[23]

Now, this assumes you're going to pay for good quality trebles and keep them razor sharp. Trebles that come on a lure when you buy it are usually fine but not always. The only problems I've had with stock trebles have been on some smaller spinners and spoons: these often come with thin-wire hooks that a big salmon can bend out. Cheaper plugs are also suspect: they might have great action, but are often hung with trebles that are too brittle and can snap when a salmon hits.

Unfortunately it's not always easy to tell if a stock treble is up to the task. Using brand-name lures usually ensures hook quality, but not always. You need to inspect them yourself. If they look suspect, change them for good brand-name trebles. Gamakatsu, Owner and Mustad make the best.

For the lures I cast, I've found that standard cut-point trebles work fine and don't cost an arm and a leg. For the snaggy-bottomed beats I usually fish, where a lure's life span rarely exceeds two hours, a little economy does make sense. But for trolling lures, which I'm often fishing from a rod stuck behind a rowlock, I feel safer using hi-tech laser cone points. They cost a bit more but they give me the little extra holding power I need to keep a fish on the line until I can pick up the rod and take over.

On some waters, fishing trebles isn't a issue – they are illegal. In such cases singles, sometimes doubles, are the default. Some lures come with these already in place, but most don't. So you may need to buy singles or doubles separately and attach them yourself. The standard is the round-bend siwash-type hook, and the gap should be bigger than that on a treble. Again, look for those made by Gamakatsu, Owner or Mustad to be certain of quality.

Matching single to treble hook sizes

Treble hook size	Single hook size
# 2	# 3/0
# 4	# 2/0
# 6	# 1 or # 2

Whether you're using singles or trebles, keep them razor sharp. Sharpen all cut points before you use them for the first time and carry a sharpening stone or hook file to the waterside for resharpening. The hi-tech Gamakatsus, Owners and Mustads won't need as much resharpening, but it's a good idea to check any hook you're using every fifteen or twenty minutes, especially if you are working over a rocky bottom. Check them also after getting loose from a snag or hooking a fish. Experienced anglers call a point sharp enough when it easily sticks to a fingernail.

One last point. Many river authorities that require or encourage catch-and-release fishing also require you to fish barbless – so you'll need to flatten all the barbs on your stock hooks using pliers.

3. Covering, Hooking, Playing and Landing Salmon

We've put together a sure-fire line-up of lures. Success is sure to follow. Not so! First, we have to face a hard reality: if a salmon can't detect or catch our lure, it doesn't matter whether it's top class or that proverbial pencil-sharpener. In fact, put a skilled angler fishing a pencil-sharpener up against a novice fishing a proven lure, and my money is on the pencil-sharpener every time. That's because covering fish is the key to success. Whoever covers the most fish, catches the most – it's as simple as that.

In this chapter I'll describe a number of techniques for presenting a lure effectively to salmon in rivers. I'll look at the best ways of fishing in warm water and cold, clear and turbid waters, under low- and bright-light conditions, and on foot or from a boat. I'll describe the different tackle set-ups you'll need and give some pointers on how best to hook, play and land salmon on spinning gear. First, some general guidelines on covering salmon with spinning baits.

Covering Salmon: Putting Your Lure in the Strike Zone

Everybody agrees that the key to taking salmon is covering them with your lure. So what does that mean, exactly? Well, it depends on the state of the water: how fast it's flowing, how clear and cold it is, and whether it's well lit or not.

First, covering a fish means putting your lure in the strike zone. That is, close enough for the salmon to detect it and possibly react to it. It's what biologists call *reaction distance*. Now, for trout (including sea trout) we estimate the distance to be about three feet on the outside – for clear, slow-moving water. This seems to fit with trout anglers' experiences; there's also some good research to back it up.[24]

For an adult salmon, the strike zone is probably bigger. Unfortunately, researchers haven't yet helped much on this question, so we need to go with anglers' impressions. Experts like Hugh Falkus have described salmon moving to lures in clear, slow currents from distances of up to about 6 ft (1.8 m). In my experience, that seems about right.[25] Whether a salmon can detect a lure further away than that isn't known, so to be safe we want to get our lure within 6 ft (1.8 m) of one to stand a chance of a take. That's not as small a target area as when fishing for trout, but still challenge enough if we are to cover a piece of water effectively.

And that's in clear water. Once water colours up, even a little, the strike zone shrinks, and the target gets smaller. There is plenty of research to back this up: turbidity in water affects reaction distance.[26] From my reading of the reports it seems the strike zone is *roughly half the distance an angler can see through the water*. So if the water is clear enough for you to see about 6 ft (1.8 m) through it, you're safe in thinking a salmon will strike a lure at about half that distance: about 3 ft (1 m) or less. If you can only see 3 ft (1 m), say your boot toes when standing waist deep, your lure will need to get closer still – under 18 in (45 cm). So, obviously, the more coloured the water, the closer the lure needs to be to elicit a strike.

So we need to put our lure inside the strike zone. But does it matter where? Some say it does. We do know a salmon only has binocular vision or depth perception right in front of it – a cone-shaped space about 30° wide. Some feel that's where a lure ought to be to have the greatest chance of getting taken. But in my experience a lure sidling up to a fish will trigger a strike just as often. So will one streaking right overhead. Certainly a lure appearing in the salmon's blind spot (a 30° cone right behind it) isn't going to get taken. Outside that, though, where in the salmon's field of vision you put the lure probably doesn't matter as much as how close you put it, how fast it's going, and what action it has.

How about light levels? I mentioned in Chapter 2 that salmon (and trout) see best in dawn- and dusk-level illumination. Darker or lighter than that, and the strike zone is going to be smaller.

Finding the Right Depth

Given the relatively small size of the strike zone – 6 ft (1.8 m) or less in running water – we need to know how deep fish are going to be to have any chance of covering them effectively with a lure. This won't always be easy. A number of factors are at play: water temperature and clarity, how bright the light is and the activity level of the fish themselves, whether they are cold or warm, resting or running. Still, from the experiences of generations of salmon anglers, along with some observations made by scientists, it's possible to make at least one useful generalization: *inactive fish lie nearer the bottom, while active fish run higher up.*[27]

Migrating salmon need to conserve energy for the rigours of spawning. One way to do this is to rest or hold near or on the river bed, where bottom contours and features like boulders can serve as refuges against the current. It's common to catch salmon whose bellies are abraded and worn from 'sitting'.

As for more active fish, running salmon tend to move upstream in a leap-frog manner: running higher up for a distance before dropping back down again to rest. In warmer water, when they are in top physical condition, they may run well above resting fish: anywhere from mid-depth to right up under the surface – higher when the water is turbid or the light low, deeper when it's clear and bright. These fish are a common sight on many streams and smaller rivers, leaping or breaking the surface as they move upstream on a warm summer's evening.

In colder water, when their metabolism is slow and their swimming ability constrained, active fish may run just above or even among resting fish, within only a few feet of the bottom. This is probably why the fishing on many rivers gets so much better once the water drops to about 45–35°F (7–1°C). Not only are there more fish concentrated near the bottom – making it easier to cover them – the fish are now more takeable too. Remember, more concentrated fish means edgier, more aggressive fish. A well placed lure is often just the kind of trouble these fish are spoiling for.

Someone once said that ninety per cent of caught fish are taken within 1 ft (30 cm) of the bottom. I don't doubt it. Given what we know about resting and running fish, many anglers have simply decided to fish deep all the time: there's always the chance of covering resting fish, and, if the water is cold enough, running fish too. It's the safe play. But there are times – namely when the water gets warm – when deep-lying fish aren't going to be our best targets, and we can increase our chances of action by going after the more active fish running higher up.

Getting the Speed Right

It's the general understanding among experienced anglers that salmon prefer a slower bait than sea trout do. Not too helpful unless you're a sea-trout fisher, I know. Hugh Falkus was a little more specific. He felt the right speed for a salmon lure (fly or spinner) was about 1½–3 mph (2.5–5 kmph), or about the swimming speed of a small bait-fish.[28] That's more helpful; it's roughly between a leisurely walking pace and a brisk one. It also happens to be just about the range of current speeds I normally fish on my local beats. I know this because I've made a habit of pacing along the water's edge for 10 yd (9 m) or so before wetting my line, so as to get an impression of the speed of the current that day. Knowing the speed of the water helps me choose lures and how best to deliver them. For example, if the current is racing along at some 3 mph (5 kmph) or more, I'll probably be fishing something slow across-current or even slower against it. If it's only lumbering along, I might want to give my lure a little more welly by working the reel crank or throttling up the harling motor (see 'Presentations' below).

Gauging lure speed

You can get a feel for how fast a lure is moving by carrying out this simple waterside exercise with your rod. Start by tossing out a lure into the water. Hold the rod nearly horizontal. Now, raise it up to 12 o'clock in one smooth action. It probably took you about one second to raise the rod from horizontal to vertical. If so, you accelerated the lure to a velocity of roughly the length-of-your-rod per second. If it's 9 ft (2.7 m), that's some 9 ft (2.7 m)/sec, or about 6 mph (9.5 kmph). Twice to three times the ideal speed for most presentations.

That doesn't mean fast-moving lures aren't effective. Some presentations – like jigging, ripping, and stop-and-go, which I'll describe below – incorporate bursts of speed way over 3 mph (5 kmph). But, most important, they also incorporate breaks in speed. The bursts of speed seem to catch the salmon's eye. But it's almost always the pausing, slowing or even dropping lure that elicits the strike.

Now, in my experience a good speed range to aim for at ideal temperatures and warmer (that is, water above say 45°F/7°C would be 1½–3 mph (2.5–5 kmph). Colder than that and we've got to compensate for our quarry's reduced metabolism, sensitivity to stimuli and reaction speed.[29] We need to slow our presentation down. In cold water, a lure that is barely moving or even hanging in the current is often the most effective.

It's the same story for turbid water, regardless of temperature. Coloured water means a shorter reaction distance and a smaller strike zone. So we will need to give our fish a little more time to react to the lure by slowing it down, so it stays within visual range longer.

A salmon of some 4 lb (1.8 kg)

This 24 lb (11 kg) fish is about twice the size of the average take

Using simple geometric patterns (such as stripes, bars, dots, diagonals and diamonds) is the easiest way to make a lure more visible to salmon when the water is less than clear

Wide-bodied or fat spoons are more buoyant than narrower, elongated spoons and better suited to fishing moderate flows, mid-pool drifts, shallow runs, slack near-shore water or when drifting with the current

Elongated or skinny spoons are less buoyant than fat spoons, so better suited to fishing across or against deep strong flows, very fast currents, or, in lighter weights, for high, fast presentations

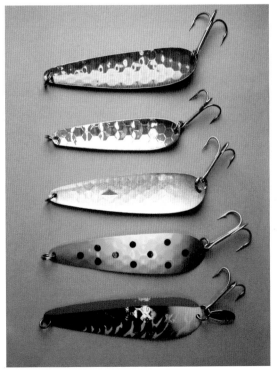

Thin-blade spoons are extremely thin, light and buoyant and, when rigged up with ledger weights, can be fished very, very slowly along the bottom or hung in a slow current without much risk of snagging

Jigging spoons are thick, compact, slab-shaped lures designed to have a seductive action when dropped vertically through the water. They are a good first choice for sink-and-draw (jigging) presentations

Conventional blade-spinners like the Mepps are ideal for high, fast retrieves with the current, because the light blade revolves (and attracts) even against low water resistance

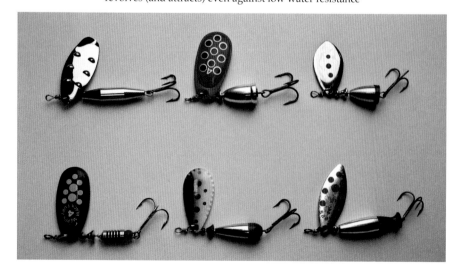

Rapala-type diving plugs are buoyant or semi-buoyant plug-shaped baits with a lip at the front, so they dive and wiggle attractively when pulled through the water. When rigged with dropper-weights they are ideal for harling

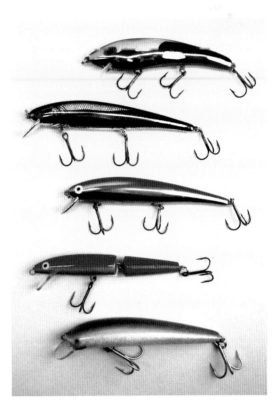

Bevelled diving plugs like J-plugs and Kynock Killers are a favourite alternative to Rapala-type plugs among harlers

Mending line by flipping the bow upstream can help keep a lure fishing deeply in the current

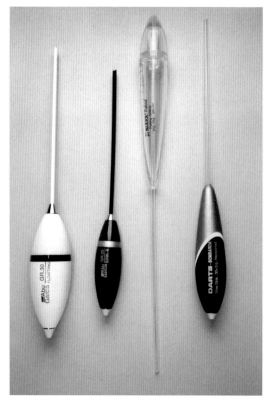

Casting bombs are a good alternative to in-line weights when fishing very light lures high in the water. They come in slow-sinking, semi-buoyant and floating models weighing from ⅜ – 1⅜ oz (10–40 g)

Keeping pressure on a hooked fish no matter what is the key to landing it

A big fish calls for a big net

Tailing a salmon. Note the angler keeps the rod bent to maintain pressure on the fish until it is well in hand

Presentations for Working Currents

Anglers have devised a range of methods for presenting spin-baits in rivers. They include flatline, ledger and float methods for fishing both on foot and from your boat. I'll describe the standard ones, along with some less well known moves worth trying.

Flatline Fishing On Foot

The first thing an angler does on the bank is decide how to rig up, whether for flatline fishing, for fishing dropper weights or for fishing floats. Flatline is standard fishing, tossing heavier non-buoyant lures as is, or with the help of some in-line weights like split shot or Wye leads to get them out and down. Most bank anglers fish with simple flatline rigging, and most salmon are probably taken that way. Here are some flatline presentations for working currents on foot.

Deep-Sweeping

This is the bread-and-butter presentation for cold-water salmon. The object is to sweep a heavy lure – usually a spoon or spinner – across the target water, keeping it within 1 ft (30 cm) of the bottom and fishing with a nice, slow, wobbling beat. Deep is where most of the fish are going to be once the water drops below 45°F (7°C) to about 30°F (-1°C), so that's where we need to fish to catch them. Master this move, and fish will soon follow.

But deep-sweeping is much harder than it looks. I learned the finer points from Stig and Renée Höglund. They are the best I've ever seen. Here's how they do it. They start by positioning themselves a little above the water they want to cover. This could be a current break not too far out, a distant pocket, a known lie, even the whole width of a glide.

Depending on how strong and deep the water is, they make the cast anywhere from a little above (10 o'clock) to a little below (2 o'clock) to straight across (12 o'clock) – so that the lure has sunk

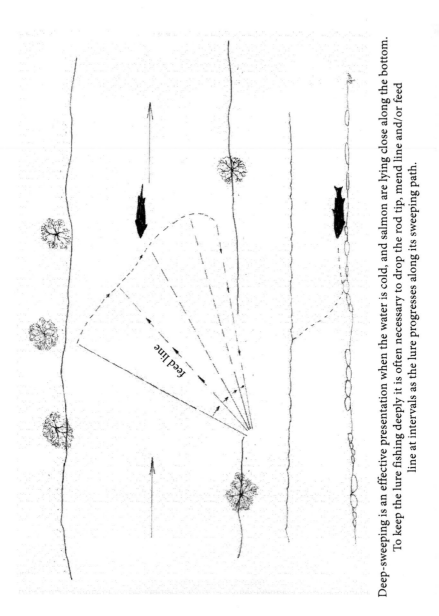

Deep-sweeping is an effective presentation when the water is cold, and salmon are lying close along the bottom. To keep the lure fishing deeply it is often necessary to drop the rod tip, mend line and/or feed line at intervals as the lure progresses along its sweeping path.

down to fishing depth (near bottom) and is moving at the right speed (and with the right action) *before* it enters the target water. They know their tackle and the currents well enough, so they rarely miscalculate. If it's all done correctly, the lure covers any fish in its sweep by entering its visual range from an oblique side angle. It's a very effective trigger, and you can expect a strike anywhere along the sweep.

One of the things I first noticed watching the Höglunds was that they hardly ever touched the crank handle. As I later learned, if you've calculated the initial casting angle right, taking into consideration current speed and depth, and if you know your tackle and how fast your lure (and line) sink, you shouldn't need to touch the reel crank at all until the lure has completed its arc down below you and you want to bring it back home. Any reeling before that and you're only going to pull that lure up too high off the bottom, over the fish's heads, and out of the strike zone. If you see an angler spinning in cold water with an active crank hand, you can be sure it's a beginner. That's why novice spinners usually take their first salmon in warm water (but more on that below).

Another thing I learned from Stig and Renée is that, for every fish you take fishing within 1 ft (30 cm) of bottom, you can take two if you keep it inside 6 in (15 cm)! Maybe that's an exaggeration, but not such a big one. In any event, that's tight fishing! It means bumping the bottom every few seconds, which is hard to do without getting yourself into trouble. But it's definitely worth the risk. At 6 in (15 cm) off bottom you're putting the lure at just about the fish's eye level. And all that bumping only makes it more detectable and attractive as a target.[30] I've seen the Höglunds take twice as many fish as everybody else on the beat put together in a single evening fishing tight along the bottom.

Does one lose lures? Yes, by the score! You get about an hour of fishing out of a lure you're bouncing along the bottom – two hours maximum.[31] But that's deep-sweeping: you lose lures, and you catch fish. Still, it doesn't need to be as expensive as it sounds. Most of us make our own spoons, so we're talking lost pennies – not pounds. The Höglunds use one home-made spoon only, which is a clue to their great skill in delivering it. It's an oval wide-body spoon about 3 in (7.5 cm) long and weighing about 1 oz (28 g). Stig makes them all himself out of soft alloy metal. The mould design is based on a local spoon (now no longer made), but it looks much like the Little Cleo of Pacific Coast fame. As for colour and patterns, he merely paints it silver all over and adds a single stripe of red-orange along the bottom (convex) edge. Simple and effective. Perfect for working the deep glides he generally fishes. On some of his older survivors the paint is pretty much worn off the underbelly from bumping along the bottom. I make my own version and call it the Mobacken after the beat where it first won me over as a good deep-sweeping spoon (see Appendix).

STAYING DEEP

The main challenge to deep-sweeping correctly is keeping the lure down throughout the sweep, since it will be fishing mostly against the current, which works to push the lure up rather than down. Remember: taking in line, no matter how slowly, only makes it worse. Experienced sweepers have several ways to keep a lure sweeping deeply. If the current isn't too strong or deep you might get away with simply dropping the rod tip as the lure progresses through the sweep. That's the Höglunds' style: rod tip high at the start of the sweep and nearly flat against the water by the end. But then, they seem to calculate their initial casting angle precisely. I've managed it on shallower stretches by plunging my rod tip right down into the water. But on deeper, stronger water I need to 'fight the push', as the great steelhead fisher Bill Herzog says, with more aggressive moves so I can stay deep and slow.

One method is feeding line. If you've got a multiplier or a fixed-spool reel with a *bait-runner* or *free-line* function,[32] you simply engage the free-spool and let the current take line in bursts whenever you feel the lure pushing up. Another is mending line. This was introduced to spinners by Bill Herzog. But it's really a page right out of the fly-angler's bible. I described this in *Spin-Fishing for Sea Trout*:

> The goal of mending is to keep a straight and more or less taut line between rod and lure. You do this by correcting the bow

that naturally builds up in the line due to the force of the current by flipping it up and back – or 'mending' it. If you don't, the bow builds up drag against the current and pulls the lure up and around in an accelerated whiplash or S course: not good.

How often you need to 'mend' will depend on the current. If you are working into a faster current fewer mends will be needed during the sweep. But if you are working from or across faster into slower water – say you are positioned on the outside of a river's bend for example – a bow will quickly develop and you will need to mend several times through the sweep. With practice mending can be combined with line feeds and together used to keep your lure sweeping along the bottom where it needs to be.

If it still won't stay down, try using a heavier lure or adding an in-line weight like a Wye lead (see 'Tackling-up for Fishing Flatline', p. 84).

You can also try slowing down your presentation by casting a longer line at a greater angle downstream and feeding line more often. This is especially useful in very cold water, where slower is always better. Using a sinking mono or one of the newer sinking braids also helps.

For deep-sweeping I use a variety of spoons and spinners depending on the water. My favourites are my homemade Mobacken and Fattail spoons (see Appendix for how to make them), and a Flying C spinner. Even heavy jigging spoons – like my own Fathead – can be perfect for sweeping in very strong, deep currents.

On many British waters deep-sweeping buoyant Devon-like minnows with the aid of small in-line leads is a standard cold-water move. Mike Taylor of the Red Lion Hotel at Bredwardine on the middle Wye was nice enough to share some of his expertise on fishing minnows:

1. Wye minnows are made of hazel wood, and therefore float, but in all other respects are the same as their heavier cousins – Devon minnows.
2. They are tied to a leader of about 18–24 in (45–60 cm) which is then attached to the main line by a ball-bearing swivel. Above

this swivel is a weight, which will vary according to the flow and depth of the water you are fishing; this keeps the minnow down and spinning just above the bottom of the river. If you can make your own weights we use Wye lead, which is banana-shaped with a wire running through it. At one end is a loop to which you tie the main line: at the other you fix the swivel to which you tie the leader. This shape of weight helps prevent getting stuck on the bottom, especially in rivers with a gravel bed.

3. The colour can vary but here on the Wye we find that a Green & Yellow is very good, also Brown & Gold. In very clear water (especially if it is very cold) I find Blue & Silver works very well.

4. Probably the best way to fish them in this country is to cast at a slight downstream angle and let the minnow arc round. On some occasions the fish will follow it and take on the dangle or just as you start to retrieve, so for the first few yards it's best not to wind in too quickly.[33]

High-Sweeping

Anytime the water is over 45°F (7°C), sweeping a lure high up is worth a go. Active running fish in top condition seem to respond well to something streaking obliquely overhead. When the water is clear and the light low – say on a cloudy day, or anytime from dusk to dawn – this presentation can really pay off. It's an especially good way to cover a pool tail, or for scouring a long glide one strip at a time (see 'Working a Grid', p. 100).

It's easy to pull off too. The manoeuvre starts out like a normal deep-sweep with the initial toss anywhere from about 10 to 2 o'clock depending on the current strength. Only now you want to keep your rod tip up so the current can hold the lure just under the surface the whole way through the sweep. If it starts to rise up to the surface as it accelerates, keep it down by dropping the rod tip, feeding line or mending.

High-sweeping seems to come naturally. In fact, it's why most novices – at least on beats I fish – seem to hook their first salmon high-sweeping on a warm summer's evening. A small spoon is cast out across the river – maybe one that's taken trout or perch for them – then slowly reeled in. The lure streaks around in a big whipping arc high in the water. Sometimes a salmon nails it.

Any small lure will do for high-sweeping in warmer conditions. But I prefer a skinny spoon, since it runs easily with little water resistance.

As for ideal depth, experts like Falkus recommended about 4 in (10 cm) below the surface for summer flies, and that's about right for spinning-baits too. But at times I've scored in semi-darkness sweeping very small lures – spoons, spinners, even Devons, no more than 1½ in (4 cm) long – right across the surface like the sea-trout fisher's wake fly.[34] To pull this off, forget about mending or feeding line and let the current pull the lure around in 'crack-the-whip' style.

Deep-Drifting

Drifting a wide-bodied spoon right along the bottom with the current is one of the best ways for taking cold-water sea trout (I describe the manoeuvre in detail in *Spin-Fishing for Sea Trout*). But I can probably count on both hands the number of times a salmon has taken my drifting lure. Most of those that did actually took it when it was making the turn at the bottom, or even coming back up on the return. Other drift anglers I've talked to admit the same: salmon rarely hit a lure drifting straight down the current at them.

On some Pacific Coast rivers, though, drifting *is* a favourite move for taking salmon when the water is running fast and clear. It's called *flipping* there and it's considered high-yield. According to PDQ Guides (http://fishing.pdqguides.com/salmon-fishing-guide.html),

> Flipping is done in faster streams than you'd use for plunking or casting. You cast the line upstream at a forty-five-degree angle to your position, and let the lure bounce its way down the flow of the water. You don't use the reel at all in this kind of fishing, but the line must never lose its tension. To do this, you need to sweep your rod slowly in an arc along the downstream path of the bait. It's important to keep the line down to the lure as straight as possible. When the lure completes its journey along

the arc, pull it out with a little jerky movement towards the bank. This will ensure that any salmon interested in your lure does get hooked before you finally pull the line in.

Why drifting works better for them than me is probably due to the different water conditions we fish. I do most of my fishing in water that's fairly fast, over 6½ ft (2 m) deep and off-coloured. A lure drifting flatline with the current is usually moving too fast to be effective. So unless I manage to hit a fish right on the nose, my lure is in and out of the strike zone before the fish can grab it. For me, a deep-sweeping lure is a more efficient and effective way to cover a piece of cold water deeply. So I tend to reserve flatline drifting for sea trout.

This doesn't apply at all to drifting with ledger weights (roll ledgering) or from a boat (back trolling) – both can be deadly under the right conditions (see below). That's because a dropper-weight or a drifting boat's motor lets you slow a lure down enough to make it an easy target for even a cold salmon.

Jigging or Sink-and-Draw

Jigging is probably one of the oldest ways of presenting a spinning bait to salmon. It used to be called *trolling* or *trowling* and meant fishing a lure with *sink-and-draw* – or jigging it. This was how that 'lure of bryte shel' in the 1,100-year-old story I mentioned in the Introduction was fished. It makes sense. Jigging a lure up and down in deep, near-shore water was the easiest way to fish it from the bank before better reels and thinner lines made longer casts possible. It worked too! It seems it's hard for salmon to resist a lure fluttering down into their lie from above. (And don't forget the early tale of salmon nailing dropped soup spoons!)

But the classic method of jigging a lure up and down vertically is of pretty limited use for working a river on foot. Deep holes and canyon-like drop-offs close to your bank are of course prime candidates. So is the water at the base of a fall or under a bridge. Vertical jigging from a drifting boat can also be very effective (see 'Fishing From a Boat: Harling', p. 109). But more commonly nowadays the sink-and-draw is worked into other presentations like sweeping or drifting[35] or backing down (see p. 80).

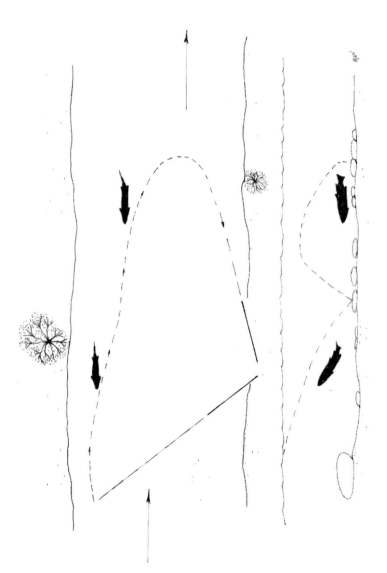

Jigging the lure up and down, or *sink-and-draw*, can be effectively worked into conventional presentations like sweeping, backing-down or, as illustrated here, drifting.

Jigging can be an effective twist to simple drifting for example, especially in cool to warm conditions, when fish are willing to chase down lures more actively. You start out the same but instead of keeping the spoon drifting along with the current you step it down by lifting the rod tip up to about 10 o'clock, then dropping it back down again, or sink-and-draw. You can jig it deep, literally bouncing it along the bottom in big steps, or keep it up high, letting it drop down to mid-depth or so before drawing it up again. Both seem to work: deeper when it's cooler, higher up when it's warmer. You can work the sink-and-draw into deep- or high-sweeping the same way.

I like the sink-and-draw because I can cover the depth of the water column more thoroughly than with straight drifting or sweeping. I might even go over a stretch twice before moving on: first deep-jigging, then high-jigging. I can also cover deeper pockets out from shore better by letting the lure sink or step-down into a hole during a drift or sweep.

But jigging has one big drawback: the risk of foul-hooking a fish (see 'Foul-hooking risk', p. 79). When a lure is working up though the water where fish are numerous, it can easily snag a salmon in the belly, side, even fins, tail or back. This is a nasty business, to be avoided the best you can. Unfortunately, if you jig long enough you'll eventually foul-hook a fish. Jigging from the bank is especially prone to this, because the jigging lure doesn't surge up vertically but at an angle. It's easy for the line to drag across the fish's back or under its belly, and guide the treble right into it – called raking. For this reason, jigging is forbidden on some rivers altogether. Even where it isn't, many anglers avoid it or only use it sparingly and with great care.

You can't eliminate the foul-hooking risk, but you can minimize it. The best way is to choose lures designed for jigging. Lots of anglers jig skinny spoons, for example. The problem is the standard spoon is top heavy. This means it turns over and drops in an erratic weaving or darting pattern. A salmon will almost always try to nail a jig on the drop. When it does, more times than not it misses. Instead it ends up with line draped or even wrapped around itself: you feel it, you tighten the line, and you unwittingly drive the hook into the fish's body somewhere. Jigging spoons –

like my own Fathead – are heavier (or have less resistance) toward the hook end. On the drop they flutter down while staying more or less upright, so a salmon can get a cleaner shot at the tail/treble hook. A skinny spoon fished in reverse can also make a good jigging lure (see 'Reversing a spoon's direction', p. 43).Whatever lure you are jigging you can also reduce the risk of foul hooking by working it in a controlled way, especially on the drop. Don't let it free fall. Instead, follow it down so the line stays in contact the whole way. This will keep the lure from turning over and falling erratically, and make it an easier target for a striking fish to grab cleanly. It's easier to stay in controlled contact with a dropping lure using monofilament, so many avid jiggers prefer it to braid.

Ripping

The first time I caught sight of an angler *ripping* a spoon was on a warm summer's evening years ago. It was Micke. From a distance, I thought he was trying to get loose from a really bad snag. With elbows akimbo and back arched, he whipped his rod up repeatedly as he followed the line downstream. I though he must have sunk his spoon into a drifting log. On the rivers we fish, it happens! But closer up I saw I was wrong: he was actually fishing. He had one fish on the bank, and was going for two. Since then I've learned to rip too, and I can say it's one of the few moves that really works on warm-water salmon.

Ripping is like jig-sweeping high in the water, only harder and faster. It's aimed specifically at fresh fish running high in the current. The theory is that these new arrivals from the sea are still vulnerable to anything that looks like one of those bait-fish they hunt in the salt. And I think there's something in it. We know that a common ploy of salmon hunting a school of fish, like herring or capelin, is to torpedo through the bunched bait-fish aiming to stun or break one. The fish scatter of course, usually racing upward at top speed toward the surface. (Sometimes from a boat you can catch sight of hunted bait-fish breaking the surface, even leaping into the air.) After the initial charge the salmon turns back to gobble up any wounded fish. These are easy to identify because typically they are *falling slowly down and away from the rest with the fluttering action of a fish in trouble.* And *that* is the scenario the ripping spoon seems to imitate.

The technique, as Micke taught it, starts out with a long cast across a big glide where lots of running fish are showing – anywhere from about 10 o'clock to 2 o'clock depending on current strength. As in sweeping, if the initial throw is right you shouldn't have to touch the crank until the spoon is hanging below you. Once the lure hits the water, you let it sink for a couple of seconds only, no more. You want to keep it *within the top 1 ft (30 cm) or so of water*, above the fish. Then, with your rod down about level to the water, give it a good rip! Don't be shy! Don't lift it up – this isn't controlled sink-and-draw jigging. Whip it up! Literally as hard and fast as you can. You're after speed here, enough so you feel that spoon break into a rapid chatter. Once the rod tip is all the way up over your head, drop it down more slowly. You want a controlled drop; ideally you want the spoon to sink with the pathetic fluttering of a wounded bait-fish. But don't stop now. After a few seconds, rip it up again.

As I said, if you've calculated the current strength correctly, you should be able to rip-and-drop the spoon around its whole course as it sweeps in a broad down-current arc, until it's hanging straight below you. Once there – at the dangle – you can reel it in quickly, or keep ripping all the way back (see 'Bringing it back home', p. 83).

Micke's standard ripping lure was a plain copper wide-bodied spoon, made locally and called the Laxy. But other spoons rip well too. What you want to look for is a spoon that tracks straight with a good chatter when accelerated – ripped – through the water. (If you feel a strong vibration from the spoon when it's ripping, you're probably onto a good one.) It may be the same spoon you fish with a nice lazy wobble on the sweep, or maybe another one.

What's important is that the spoon breaks into a fast chatter on the upsurge, because that's what's going to catch the attention of any edgy, keyed-up warm-water runner nearby. But any takers won't hit it then. They'll almost always wait for the spoon to stop and start to fall down toward them from overhead. So the most effective ripping spoons also have a nice fluttering action on the drop.[36] But watch out for spoons that dart and roll erratically at high speeds. They attract salmon too, but they can be too hard for a near-sighted fish to nab, so they often evade capture or only achieve a poor hook-up.

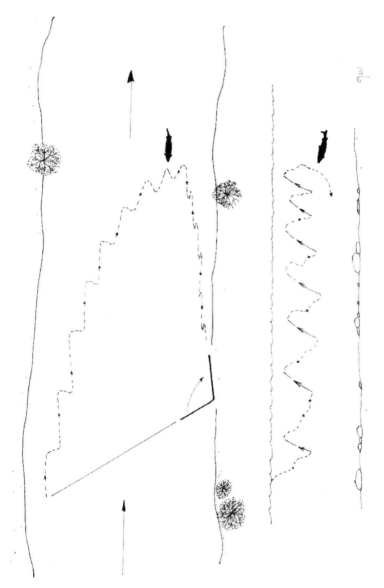

Ripping is like jigging a lure high in the water, only with much greater speed and force. It can be especially effective on fresh, running salmon under very warm conditions.

As for coverage, you've got a couple of options. One is scouring the holding water thoroughly by casting to a mental grid. The other is targeting (see 'Working a Grid', p. 100). Most experienced rippers I know like to rip down a river – a big glide is perfect – one strip at a time. They make the cast across, all the way to the other bank if they can, rip the spoon through its arcing course back home, then move down a few paces and rip off another strip.

This is active, mobile fishing, and a great way to cover a stretch of river quickly looking for any game salmon. It takes up a lot of space though, and unless you're alone it can really irritate other, non-ripping anglers. If several of us are ripping together, fine, then we simply move on down the beat in unison, everybody following the same routine. I've even pulled it off among non-rippers once they understood I was only fishing the top 1 ft (30 cm) of water, and only passing through. But this takes more charity from my fellow anglers than I'm normally willing to ask. So if I'm too hemmed in for mobile ripping, I might turn to targeted ripping instead.

TARGETED RIPPING

This is just what it sounds like: targeting running fish. Sometimes you can actually see the fish, as it moves up under the surface and back down. But it's usually the surface splash or the aerial display you glimpse from the corner of your eye. The sport now is to place your spoon just above and a little in front of where you think that fish will be in the next few seconds. Remember, we're still talking about a target area – the strike zone – with no more than a 6 ft (1.8 m) radius. So precision does count. If you find a good piece of water where many salmon are showing, you can stand all evening 'target shooting'. I caught my first ripped salmon this way, a 24 lb (11 kg) hen on a black, orange and gold 1 oz (28 g) Abu Koster, in 61°F (16°C) water on an August evening at 9 o'clock. It was probably the most thrilling fight I've experienced, and the toughest fighter. She seemed to be out of the water more than in, and stripped most of the line off my reel on a couple of runs.

Ripping is violent stuff; not for the meek or the weak. But, if you're up for it, it can pay off when other methods leave you flat. A word of caution, though. When ripping by the book isn't working, it's natural to start ripping deeper and deeper – to get closer to the fish, you think. *Don't do it!* It's a sure recipe for foul hooking. And believe me: belly-hooking a salmon is about as unpleasant an experience as you'll ever have fishing (see box below).

Foul-hooking risk

When a fish has got hooked even though it didn't take the lure, it's called *foul hooking*. It's illegal everywhere to foul-hook or snatch a fish deliberately. If you fish long enough, though, you will eventually foul-hook one unintentionally. It's a nasty business, but it's inevitable. What constitutes a *foul-hooked*, as opposed to a *fair-hooked*, fish varies from place to place. In some areas it's any fish hooked outside the mouth. In other areas it's a fish hooked behind the gill plates (which allows for the fact that a striking fish sometimes misses taking the hook cleanly but gets hooked – fairly – outside the jaw).

To make foul hooking less likely, most fishing codes prohibit the use of hooks with gapes beyond a certain width, or jigging as a method, or fishing after dark (when poachers operate). Bank fishing is more prone to the problem than boat fishing, because lines are usually crossing over and under fish at an oblique angle and can lead the lure into the fish's belly, back or fins.

It's pretty easy to recognize when you've foul-hooked a fish. It is nearly impossible to turn or control; it feels heavy – more like a log than alive; it doesn't roll much, never jumps, and tends to run in straight courses (and, when it does run, your rod tip often shakes erratically).

The best and really only thing to do if you've foul-hooked a smaller fish is get it in as fast as you can; try to keep it in the water while getting the hook out using pliers; then release it. (It's also illegal to keep a foul-hooked fish). If it's too big to control, it's better to cut the line close off before the fish is too spent to recover. The chances are the hook will pull or drop out eventually.

Upstreaming

This is another move – like drifting – that hooks me more sea trout than salmon. But it's worth having in the arsenal for times when you're looking for a way to cover a piece of fairly shallow, clear water – like a pool neck – in daylight when it's not too cold, even warm, and fish are edgy and easily spooked. In upstreaming you work the target water from well below the fish and out of sight. Typically, a long line is thrown up above the lies and brought back downstream a little faster than the current speed and high in the water. Be careful not to let it go too deep or you'll run the risk of jagging, even foul-hooking fish. (For that reason, some waters discourage or forbid upstreaming a lure altogether.) High and fast is what you're after. You want your lure to cover any fish on an overhead diagonal crossing pattern. It's about the only presentation where you get to use the reel actively.

Small spoons and spinners are good choices for the job, but even a small Devon minnow will work with the aid of a few split shot or an in-line sinker. Hugh Falkus liked to upstream a small Mepps for hooking grilse on the down-side of a spate – once the water had lost most of its colour. He warned against tightening on a fish too savagely though, and for good reason. When a missile-like salmon slams a lure that's moving fast in the opposite direction, leaders can break! Used to setting the hook quick and hard on sea trout, I had to learn this lesson the hard way. So, easy does it; a salmon rarely needs your help setting the hook, and never when it's nailed an upstreamed lure. All you want to do is keep the line tight, and enjoy the ride!

(see 'Hooking, Playing and Landing Fish on Foot', p. 101).

Backing Down

This is essentially stepping a lure backwards straight down-current below you. It's what shrimpers call drift-lining (see Falkus 1984, p. 399). This is a good way to work a lure down through the neck of a pool or a break in the current; when the water is clear and low, it's also a good way to cover edgy fish while keeping out of sight by fishing a very long line from upstream.

Upstreaming allows the angler to cover fairly shallow clear-water lies without spooking edgy fish, by making long casts from well below the target water. Unlike sweeping, the lure covers fish diagonally on a high course more or less with, and a little faster than, the current.

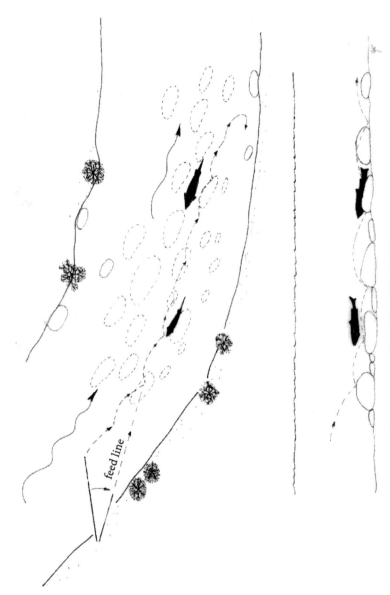

feed line

Backing down is essentially stepping a lure straight down-current below you. It's an effective way to cover a pool neck, or current break from a position above it, like the outside bend of the stream.

Positioning is the key. I like to get myself more or less straight upstream of the target. I wade out if I can, or position myself on the bank on the outside of a bend in the current. A long rod makes positioning easier, and braid line makes it easier to control the lure and to respond to a take more quickly at longer distances.

Falkus liked backing down a diving plug (a Heddon River Runt) for warm-water salmon. But you can back down almost any lure. The trick is to find one that's buoyant enough so you can back it down in steps by lifting it up, then dropping it down. Fat spoons and lighter spinners work well. So do Devons, and thin-blade spoons with the help of an in-line sinker.

Bringing It Back Home

So, you've pulled off a nice presentation, and now the lure is hanging downstream below you on the dangle. What next? Some anglers simply reel in at top speed and think about the next cast. So do I sometimes, when targeting sea trout, because maximizing drift time is often the best tactic. Not so for salmon. The home stretch is prime taking water for running fish that have pulled over to rest. So it's always worth working over carefully, especially during the twilight hours, when even the very shallow currents close to the bank can hold fish.

What's the best way to cover it? That depends on what you've been doing hitherto. In my experience it's usually best to carry on doing the same thing until your lure is up and out. If you're upstreaming fast and high, keep it going right around the bend and back home, but don't let it stall. If you're lucky a fish will follow it back, and take it right at your feet. So be ready! The same goes for ripping, sweeping, jigging, and so on: just keep it up until your lure's back home.

If that's not working, there are couple of other moves worth trying. One is simply letting the lure hover at the dangle before cranking it in, or *hanging it*. This can be a very effective way to intercept fish running up a near-bank current break. But you need to position yourself correctly: straight upstream if you can, either by wading out into the current, or finding a point along the bank on the outside bend of the river. Here's where a long rod helps. But *hanging* it takes patience.

Some anglers can hang a lure for endless minutes or as long as they can keep their lure suspended in the current. I get an itchy reel finger after about twenty seconds. Either way it's worth the time.

Another trick is *inching home*: bringing your lure back up from the dangle in tiny little steps. I tend to pump it in, holding my rod low and flat, by swivelling my body – i.e. pump, then reel in; pump and reel; pump and reel – until it's back. I've found *inching* to be most effective at very slow speeds when the water is cold, from 35–45°F (1–7°C). A warmer water version of this is *stop-and-go*. It's like *inching*, except now you're pumping your lure back a couple of feet at a time, and at a faster pace. I tend to reserve it for water that's a little warmer, over 45°F (7°C).

Tackling-up for Fishing Flatline

Like many spin-anglers, I like fishing flatline, because the rigging is simple, and there are no heavy sinkers to interfere with touch. All you need is a lure, a leader (run off your main line via a swivel, to prevent line twist) and your trusty rod and reel, and off you go.

Leader

Some anglers attach lures directly to the line. That's a mistake; it's always better to use a monofilament leader between a swivel and the bait. First, you can control breaks in the line. Using a mono leader with a slightly lower breaking strain than the main line ensures that any break occurs in the leader – usually at one of the knots – and not somewhere up the main line. Second, it protects a braid line. Braid is more brittle, more easily frayed and weakened by use, and more likely to give way when it's a little worn or damaged than mono is. A mono leader keeps a braid line from getting as battered on rocky bottoms, or a salmon's rasping teeth, and makes for tougher terminal tackle altogether. Third, mono has much more give than most braids do, so it serves as a shock-absorber for those really savage takes. Last, mono is much easier to tie and untie than braid, so lure changes are quicker.

As for attaching lure to leader, you've got two options: tying directly to the lure, or indirectly through a snap or snap swivel. I always tie on my lures directly, using a loop knot. It's simple, I don't loose more hardware than I need to when the leader breaks, and I know the lure will have all the room it needs up front to maintain the action it should. Snaps and snap swivels do make changing a lure easier, but they can dampen the action of some spoons and diving plugs. So, if you are going to use them, keep an eye on your lure's action. If it seems too cramped, try a loop knot instead.

For the leader/line connection, use any high quality swivel. The ball-bearing type is the best. But barrel swivels work just as well for bank fishing. I save the more expensive ball-bearing swivels for trolling, where I really need them.

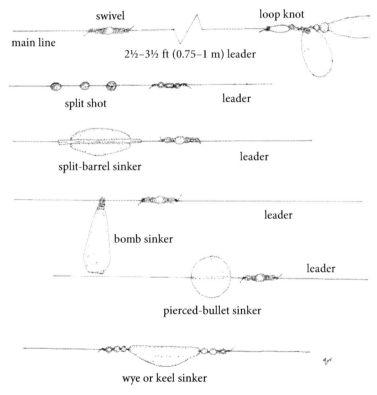

When tackling-up for flat line fishing it's best to tie the lure to a leader of 2½–3½ ft (0.75–1 m) with a loop knot, then to join leader to main line via a swivel. Any in-line sinkers should be attached to the main line above the swivel.

Leader length? Something in the region of 2½–3½ ft (0.75–1 m) is pretty common. Some prefer longer, when the water is dead clear and warm, especially if using a mainline of opaque braid. As for breaking strain, 15–25 lb (6.8–11.3 kg) mono is adequate. Some go thinner – down to 10–12 lb (4.5–5.4 kg) when the water is clear and warm.[37] I like to stay above 20 lb (9 kg). It lets me get fish in more quickly, so they have a greater chance of recovering if released, and it gives me a better chance of recovering at least some of my bottom-snagged lures. In my experience, salmon don't seem to be put off by a thick leader – at least nothing up to about 30 lb (13.5 kg) mono.

In-line Weights

Ideally, flatline presentations rely on the weight of the lure alone for casting distance and depth. But sometimes it's necessary to add a small in-line weight. Common wisdom says this shouldn't exceed the weight of the lure, or you'll get tangled when you cast. Now, I routinely cast light buoyant lures like Devon minnows, plugs, even thin-blade spoons with the help of an in-line sinker of greater weight. Sometimes it works fine, sometimes the lure wraps back on the mainline and I've got a problem. I figure it's worth the extra hassle to expand my range of offerings beyond heavy spoons and spinners. It usually is.

As for in-line sinkers, there are several standards including split shot, pierced bullet, bomb, split-barrel with stopper, and Wye/keel types. All attach to the main line above the swivel, or to the swivel itself. Most come in weights up to about 1½ oz (40 g). Each has its good and bad sides. Split shot are easy to squeeze on the line with pliers, but hard to get off. The pierced bullet slides on and off easily but rides up the line when you're casting. The Wye type is hard to find fault with – it's even got the swivel built in – but it's hard to replace if you're fishing outside Britain. My favourite is the Catherine type. It's a split-barrel you slip on to the line and hold in place with a plastic stopper. It's easy to take on and off, or reposition, and there is no need to cut or retie anything. The only downside is that, sooner or later, you lose the pin. I can usually make a replacement from a scavenged twig or wood splinter.

Casting Bombs

Several companies make buoyant or semi-buoyant in-line bombs, usually called casting bombs. They are typically plastic. You slide them on the main line above the leader and swivel and hold them in place with a long pin. Abu makes one of the best. It comes in slow-sinking, semi-buoyant and floating models weighing from ⅓–1½ oz (10–40 g). They slide on easily, cast well, and go through the water with less resistance than most.

Main Line

Whether you choose mono or braid, go for the best quality line you can afford. Pick one that's a little stronger than your leader – by at least 2 lb (1 kg). That way, any breaks will occur on the leader and not further up the line.

Some anglers fish one high quality main line all year round. Others change them seasonally. For summer fishing, when I'm mainly working small lures high in the water, I like to use a good floating braid like Berkley PowerPro or Fireline. In 25 lb (11.3 kg) test strength it's still thin enough that I can easily cast lures down to about ⅓ oz (10 g) without in-line leads or casting bombs. It's also easier to mend than sinking line. For fishing in colder weather, when I'm mainly fishing bigger lures deep, I use a sinking line. If it's above freezing, Stren Sinking Braid works nicely. But once it gets colder I switch to mono, because it accumulates less ice.

Fishing On Foot With Dropper Weights

Flatline presentations are easiest to pull off in rivers with not-too-snaggy bottoms. With plenty of practice, you *can* get really good at working over snaggy bottoms too. But many anglers turn instead to rigging that will let them stay deep while minimizing the risk of snagging, either by holding a buoyant lure down with dropper weights, or keeping a heavier lure up off the bottom via a float rig.

Roll Ledgering or Bottom-bouncing

It was probably bait anglers who first came up with a way to fish buoyant or semi-buoyant baits – like shrimp, prawn, squid or worm – very, very slowly close along the bottom with the help of a dropper weight. They call it *roll ledgering*. But it's easy enough to adapt to hardware. I've used it successfully for years fishing thin-blade spoons, Devons, even diving plugs.

You can roll ledger a lure any time. But it's an especially nice trick to pull out of the bag when the water is high and coloured, or very cold. In both situations our best hopes of a take will rest on a lure fishing deep and very, very slowly – sufficiently slowly to stay inside the strike zone long enough for a fish to see it and respond. That's where the dropper weight comes in. You keep the bait's speed down – usually just *under that of the current* – by allowing the weight to drag or hop along the bottom and act as a brake.

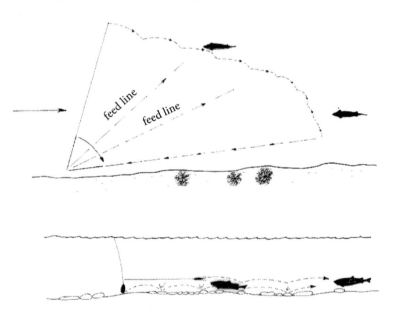

Roll ledgering, or bottom-bouncing, is an effective method of fishing a lure very slowly along the bottom, especially in very cold or coloured water. The trick is braking the lure's down-current speed by bouncing the dropper weight along the bottom.

That's the key: braking the lure's speed through the drag of the weight, while the much lighter lure is held just off the bottom by the current.

You fish the ledger rig just as if you were flatlining, only *it's the sinker, not the lure* that keeps you in touch with the bottom. It's your bottom-feeler and your speed indicator. You can fish it a number of ways. You can let the current trundle the sinker across in a sweeping arc (*ledger sweeping*); step it down and across by lifting the weight at intervals and feeding line (*ledger drifting*); or step it up and across by lifting and taking in line at intervals. You can also back it down (*backing down*) in steps from directly upstream. With a dropper set-up you can manoeuvre your lure in relation to structures, current breaks, or any piece of target water – only at a much slower, controlled speed.

Tackling-up for Roll Ledgering

The basic set-up is a three-way swivel connecting the line to the leader-and-bait, with a dropper weight run off the side swivel.

LINE AND SWIVEL

Some anglers use a sliding swivel (see under 'Ledger Plunking', below), but a stationary swivel is better, because it makes it easier to bounce your lead along the bottom. Some buy these; some assemble them by attaching two simple swivels and one snap swivel to a single split ring. For main line and leader you can go with your normal flatlining choices.

DROPPER

As for the dropper weight, you want it just heavy enough to bounce or lightly drag along the bottom *by the strength of the current alone*. You'll need to experiment, but 1–3 oz (28–85 g) is usually enough. Here are a few of the more common choices:

1. Bomb link. This is simple to rig up but more snag-prone than some others. Tie the bomb lead or similar lead-free sinker to the side swivel by a short – say 6 in (15 cm) – piece of mono. It's a

good idea to use a breaking strain less than that of the leader, so if it gets hopelessly snagged you'll only loose the sinker.

2. Split (swan) shot/loop-dropper. A little less snag-prone than a bomb link. Loop a short piece of mono through the side swivel and pinch on as many shot as you need. Start with too few and add them until the total weight is just right for the current. Some fishers hang the dropper off the rod side of a simple two-way swivel, which is one way to convert your flatline rig for fishing a dropper in a hurry. Caution: some fisheries restrict the use of shot of certain sizes/weights, so check first.

3. Pencil lead and silicon tubing. This consists of a short piece of silicon tubing attached to the swivel, and a solid or hollow length of lead or tungsten pushed into the end. It's got relatively low snag potential and good bottom 'feel'. You adjust the weight by cutting off pieces of the 'pencil'. You can get these ready-made in a range of weights, but some anglers buy the tubing and pencils separately. To attach, push the snap on a snap swivel through one end of the tubing or punch a hole through one end for tying to the side loop of a stock three-way swivel, or the rod side of a simple two-way swivel.

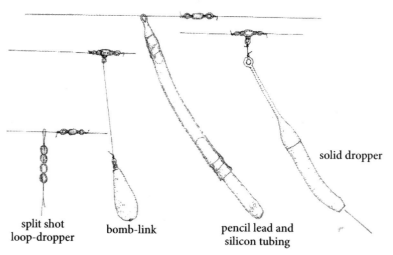

solid dropper

split shot
loop-dropper · bomb-link · pencil lead and
silicon tubing

Dropper-weight rigs answer the problem of fishing a lure deep and slow without hanging up on a snaggy bottom, whether casting from shore or harling from a boat.

4. Solid droppers. Definitely my favourite: easy to use and effective. The one-piece design is a long plastic stem with an eye for attaching to a swivel, a heavy tungsten body, and the added feature of a flexible steel needle protruding from the bottom that helps it bump along even the snaggiest bottoms without much trouble. These are less easy to get hold of but worth the search.

Ledger Plunking

This is basically roll ledgering without the roll – it's what bait anglers simply call ledgering, and what anglers across the Atlantic call plunking. You can use the same lures you do for bottom-bouncing: thin-blade spoons, diving plugs, Devons, etc. The crux of it involves casting your terminal gear into some likely holding water and allowing it to anchor there and fish in the current. The rod is placed in a holder and the angler sits back and waits for a fish to run across the lure and take it. After a while, the operation is moved to another likely spot.

Since plunking doesn't rely on broad coverage, selecting the right water to target is critical to success. On larger rivers, plunkers often set up on the inside curves to intercept any fish migrating up the current break along the inner edge of the faster water outside. On smaller rivers, the rig is sometimes cast into the neck or tail of a pool.

But plunking finds its true value when conditions are so poor that other methods seem futile. That is, when the water is running high and coloured with only 1 ft (30 cm) or so of visibility – too dirty to make most flatline presentations worth the effort. Under these conditions anchoring a big thin-blade spoon in a current break near the bank, or a big diving plug in a slackish pocket can sometimes score a running or resting salmon when nothing else will.

To place your rig, start by making a cast up above the target water. Once the weight bottoms out, step it down as you would when roll ledgering (see above) until it's where you want it. Then place the rod in a holder. If it's a wobbling lure, make sure it's keeping the right lazy action by the force of the current alone. You should be able to feel it in your hands before you put the rod down; once it's set in the holder keep an eye on the tip for updates. With experience you'll learn which lures work best in which currents. In my experience Devons work best in moderate flows, thin-blade spoons and diving plugs in the slacker water.

Plunking is passive fishing. It takes waiting and a lot of patience – more than many anglers, myself included, can muster for more than a short time. For those of us who need to keep active, one solution – where it's legal – is to fish a couple of rods. One rod is set in a holder, plunking away in a likely spot; one is in your hand, rigged for casting to other targets nearby while you keep an eye (or an ear) on the plunking rod. (Some plunkers attach a little bell on the stationary rod so they can tell when a fish has shown interest.) As I'll explain below (see 'Hooking, playing and landing fish on foot', p. 101), this isn't as risky as it sounds. Waiting is usually the best policy anyway when it comes to setting the hook in a salmon. In fact, some experienced plunkers like British Columbia's Steve Kaye say you should let a fish pull the rod down *at least three times* before picking it up and setting the hook.

Tackling-up for Ledger Plunking

Veteran plunkers use heavier tackle than flatliners. But you set up in much the same way as you do for bottom-bouncing.

SWIVEL AND LEADER

You can use a stationary three-way swivel (see above), but a sliding swivel is the better choice. To rig one up, you simply string the loop end of a snap swivel with bomb link on the main line above a regular two-way swivel. Some string a bomb weight right on the main line and use it as a slider – even simpler, but it doesn't give you any break-away protection. Either way, the slider connection keeps you in more direct contact with the lure, so you can keep closer track of things like your lure's action or a salmon's take, even when the rod is in a holder. For the leader 4–6 ft (1.25–1.75 m) of 20–40 lb (9–18 kg) mono is typical.

DROPPER

For the dropper, most plunkers go with the simple bomb type. Pyramid, bell, pancake, cannonball or bomb styles are all used. As for weight, whatever keeps your rig in place is what is needed; anything up to about 8 oz (225 g) is usual. Plunkers also use a longer dropper line than bouncers – usually 18–30 ft (5.5–9 m) of, say, 15 lb (7 kg) mono.

MAIN LINE

A mono or preferably super braid of 40–60 lb (18–27 kg) breaking strain is the norm.

Fishing On Foot With Floats: Float or Bobber Fishing

This side of the Atlantic, fishing with floats is variously called trotting, stret-pegging or laying on. It's a favourite way of presenting natural baits like worms or shrimp at long range in low, clear glides and pools without disturbing the lies. Leave it to the Pacific Coast anglers to adapt this to fishing hardware! On some rivers in Washington and British Columbia float or bobber fishing, as it's called, is the most popular method of taking steelhead trout and salmon on spinning tackle. The reason is control. A float rig lets you fish a non-buoyant lure, like a spoon or spinner, right down near the bottom more slowly than you could fishing it flatline. And, as many have found, it's a good way to learn about the river's bottom contours, obstructions and hopefully choice salmon lies. The 'poor man's depth-finder', some have called it.[38]

Float or bobber fishing is usually reserved for small to medium-size rivers in slow to medium-fast currents when the water runs clear and not too deep. Advocates say it's deadly because it lets you drift your bait with or across the current at any depth you want in a controlled but natural way. For hardware baits, light spinners are traditional first choices. But I've also fished thin-blade spoons under a float by adding a little in-line sinker to the leader a couple of feet above. Theoretically, you can fish a lure through the whole repertoire of flatline presentations using a float rig. But here are some of the better-known techniques.[39]

Free Floating

This is essentially trotting or drifting your lure down a slow to medium-fast current. You want to set the float so the bait is suspended just above bottom – at a fish's eye level. You'll need to experiment, first setting it so the lure bottoms out, then shortening up a little. Start by casting slightly upstream, then follow the bobber with your rod tip as it moves down with the current. It's important to let it drift without resistance. You'll need to be able to feed line freely once the rig passes you and moves downstream. Open the clutch on your multiplier or bait-runner fixed-spool, or the bail arm on your fixed-spool reel. You should be able to feel the lure knock the bottom every few seconds. You can let it drift down as far as you want before engaging the reel; letting the bait swing round, and reeling in. A floating braid line is more sensitive and responsive and lets you stay in better control of a long line, so most floaters prefer that over mono. As in drifting, the take is often very soft; the lure simply stops. But wait for a few tugs before setting the hook.

Down-and-across

This is the floater's rendition of stret-pegging. It's sweeping a float rig through shallower pool tails and riffles less than a few feet deep where a dead-drifting lure (see below) might hang up too often. You make the cast upstream and beyond the target water, but reel in any slack line. Once the float is across from you, free-spool it as in free floating (above). But here you want to keep just enough drag on the line so the float and lure fish diagonally across the target water in a big slow sweep. Do this by keeping your thumb on the freed-up drum of your multiplier, or the line coming off your bait-runner fixed-spool reel. On a conventional fixed-spool reel, loosen the clutch and let the current drag out line. Because your lures will be working against greater water resistance than in free floating, it will ride higher up off the bottom; to keep it fishing deep you'll need to set the float, say, 3–6 in (8–15 cm) higher (deeper) on the line (see below). Or you can try using a heavier lure or adding an in-line weight to the leader. Keep an eye on your lure's action. If it's the same spinner you used free-floating, make sure it's not spinning too fast; if it is, change to a bigger spinner or a different blade.

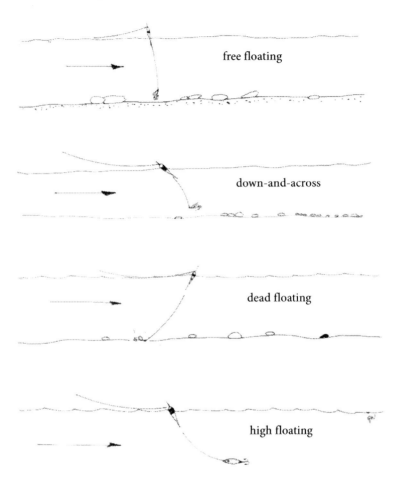

By adjusting the length of line between float and bait an angler can cover a piece of target water via free floating/trotting, down-and-across/stret-pegging, dead floating, or high floating.

Dead Floating

In both free floating and down-and-across the lure moves along near bottom, ahead of the float on the surface. With dead floating the lure is actually dragged and bounced along the bottom by the float ahead of it. This is a good ploy for picking up bottom-hugging fish in very cold water. British Columbia guide Vic Carrao discovered it by accident, watching another angler getting lucky with steelhead in mid-January. But I can tell you from experience it's just as effective on cold-river salmon. Carrao described it as follows:

> This fellow angler was fishing above me and had been there for a short time. I had noticed that he was snagging bottom frequently, his float was almost laying down flat in the water, not free-floating through the slot like most anglers would. Ten minutes passed, and I was ready to move on, when a sudden burst of water broke the silence. 'Fish on!' he yelled. This was the first of six fish this gentleman had on. The lucky angler, whose name I don't recall, had never hooked a steelhead and was experiencing the day of his life. I managed to hook a 12 lb (5.5 kg) steely on wool by the time he had his fourth fish on. I sat down and watched him for a while trying to figure out what was taking place in front of me. He was using a large No. 5 brass Colorado [spinner] under a float rig. His float was set 12 in (30 cm) deeper than the water he was fishing, therefore he was consistently snagging bottom. He would lift his rod tip to unhook the snag, then drop it, and the float would stop, then lift and stop again. Every third time he lifted to unsnag: 'Fish on!' I soon realized what was happening. By getting snagged the blade would stop turning. When he lifted his rod tip to unsnag the blade, it would turn four or five times, then stop. The action he was creating was a slow blade action. I'm convinced he had no idea why he was doing so well, and probably didn't care. I quickly changed over to a No. 5 brass blade, set my float 6 in (15 cm) deeper than the water and proceeded to fish this method. After landing four more steelhead I soon realized he was on to something. During that season I managed to hook a total of fifteen steelhead using this dead-floating method.

Freeing snags

Dead floating can be effective; potentially costly, too, in snagged and lost lures. But here's another place a bobber can help: in freeing snags. Try letting out a long line, so the bobber drifts well downstream of the snagged lure. The water drag on the bobber and long line often manages to pull the lure free. You can generally apply the same principle by means of an 'otter' – a simple float device that you snap on the line. You can buy these, but it's easier to make one by tying a paperclip or snap swivel to a dry wooden stick or a plugged bottle. Simply clip it to the line, let it slide down until it's well below the snag, then give a sharp pull until the bait comes free.

High Floating

Standard float fishing targets deeper fish. But you can also target higher runners by simply shortening the float setting so the lure rides higher up. It's a good way to fish heavy lures like spoons higher in the water; or as an alternative to your regular flatline or ledger methods for hanging or backing down a lure in a current break.

Tackling-up for Float Fishing

Learning to fish a float effectively is challenging. By all the experts' accounts the real devil is in the tackle details. It can be really simple or more involved. The basic set-up is a flatline rig with bobber added above the swivel to keep your bait-fishing at a predetermined depth.

LINE AND SWIVEL

For line and leader, a typical combination is a floating low-stretch superbraid line, a simple two-way swivel and – for the leader – 2½–3½ ft (0.75–1 m) of a sinking mono of 10–15 lb (4.5–7 kg) breaking strain.

FLOATS

Choosing floats and rigging them up is critical to success. If you are fishing water no more than say 6–8 ft (2–2.5 m) deep, all you really need is a standard fixed bobber. Plastic, cork, balsa, or Styrofoam will do. Even your casting bomb would work at a pinch. Simply attach it to the line (above your swivel) at the desired fishing depth and go to work.

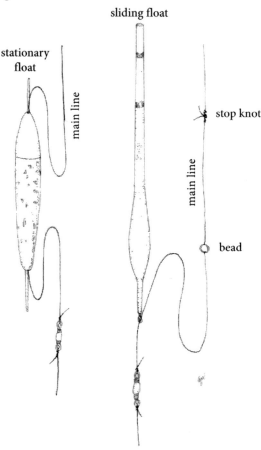

Floats are normally positioned above the swivel on the main line. On the left is a traditional stationary cork float. On the right is a wooden sliding float (note the bead and stop-knot located further up the main line).

It's also important to match float buoyancy with lure weight. You'll need to try different float types and sizes. Choose one that sits low on the water: it's easier to detect a strike on a bobber that sits no more than an inch or so above the surface than on one that sits higher. Hollow plastic floats you fill with water to adjust buoyancy are worth trying. As for size, the smallest float that still works is best; it drags less and won't put off edgy fish. As regards shape and colour, go for whatever lets you see the float well against the water at a good distance. Some like the old red-and-white, some fluorescent orange and black. Falkus suggested a more natural colour, like olive or yellow-brown, for the underwater part of the float, which he felt would appear to a fish like any piece of flotsam (1984, p. 356). He also avoided bright glossy finishes that might flash too much when cast.

SLIDER AND BOBBER STOP

All the above is for fishing shallow water where you've got ample room to cast. What about deeper water, or casting from somewhere cramped? A fixed float won't do. How do you reel in past the float when it's set deeper than rod length? How do you cast when there isn't room to whip out eight feet of terminal rigging? The answer is a sliding or running bobber with a bobber stop. The bobber stop is used to set your depth. You simply place it above the bobber at the desired depth with a bead in between. When you reel in, the stop passes through the rod guides, while the bead and float slide freely all the way down to the swivel. You can buy bobber stops pre-tied, or you can make them yourself. The standard home-made stop is simply a knot of 15 to 30 Dacron tied straight onto the line (see p. 128 for the knot); a knotted and trimmed rubber band also works. The sliding rig allows you to cast the whole package out on a few feet of line, no matter how deep you've set your float and even where casting room is limited. It also lets you land a fish on a shorter line than you could using a fixed float.

Working a Grid

Sometimes you're targeting specific pieces of likely holding water, even individual fish. But sometimes you're not: you may not know exactly where in some stretch of water a fish is going to be lying or running, so you're fishing blind. This is when your best chance of a take will come through covering as much water as you can. The best way of doing that is to cast to a mental grid. It helps you fish a piece of water systematically and thoroughly. It's better than random chucking, because you avoid dragging – raking – your line across fish before your lure covers them, and you don't leave as many gaps unfished.

Your can fit any presentation to a grid system, but sweeping (or jig sweeping) is the easiest and most efficient. Start with short casts, so that you cover the near water first. Visualize the intended path of the lure and fish it out from start to finish. The key to good coverage is spacing the casts but not changing the position from which you cast: make each cast a little further out, and on the same

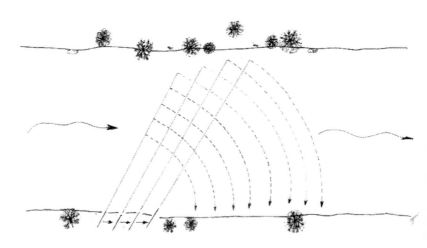

When fishing to a mental grid, one covers the water thoroughly by spacing casts at intervals no wider than the salmon's strike zone: usually 3 ft (1 m) or less.

line. I like to pick a target on the far bank, a bush or rock say, and aim at that. But watch the spacing; the next cast should never exceed the last by more than a salmon's strike zone: 6ft (1.8 m) at the most – and if the water is coloured or dark, then less.

Hooking, Playing and Landing Fish On Foot

As for hooking their fish, salmon anglers have – unlike sea trout fishers – probably lost more fish by striking (setting the hook) too soon than by striking too late. The code of the sea trout angler is: if you feel anything that could be a fish, set the hook – in waterside parlance, 'Jerk or be one!' In sea trout fishing the fastest hands often take the most fish. Not so in salmon spinning. If you want to hook salmon it's almost always better to *wait for the fish to make the first move*. After months of sea trout fishing it usually takes me a few encounters with salmon to relearn the lesson; I often lose them until I've tamed my instinctive hook-setting reflex.

How long to wait to strike a salmon depends on the kind of take. Sometimes there is no question. A fish slams the lure, the rod bows over, and the fish is off running or sailing through the air. That fish is either well hooked or it isn't; there's nothing much you can do to influence it either way. Lean back, keep the pressure on, and hope your hook hold lasts the fight.

That's the easy scenario, the *slam*. If yours is a charmed life, all your takes will be like that. But usually it's not so clear-cut. Sometimes, a salmon seems reluctant to hit a lure, so it hits it half-heartedly, so to speak. Result: the so-called *short take*. In my experience, this is more prevalent under warm summer conditions when fish are edgy. Frustrating too, to feel your lure knocked, or nipped, or even taken hold of momentarily, then dropped. Short-takers are tough customers. But striking fast isn't the answer. About the only moves worth trying with these fish are going with a smaller lure; maybe tying some yarn on the hook; even pulling out an old fly-fisher's trick and rigging up a trailing stinger hook.

Add a stinger for short-takers

One of the fly-angler's oldest tricks for taking fish that come short is to add a small flying treble hook on a short extension off the main fly – *a stinger*. Spin-anglers can do the same to a spoon or spinner. Try tying a treble wrapped with coloured yarn behind the main hook, attaching it to the rear split ring using a short piece of monofilament. Or remove the main hook altogether and attach the stinger alone. Anglers have different opinions on how far behind the lure body a stinger should ride: some say 1–2 in (2.5–5 cm), some 1 ft (30 cm) or more. Experiment.

A salmon can also take a lure very softly, even hold it in its 'lips' for a couple of seconds before dropping it or clamping down on it. This is more typical of takes when drifting, backing down, or back trolling a bait. You feel a stop, a thump, sometimes a crunching or rasping vibration, as the salmon 'tooths' the lure. *Don't strike*, whatever you do! Migrating salmon develop hard, bony mouths. It's almost too easy to snatch a lure clean away from a fish before it's

Yarn ties for better hook-ups

Many American anglers tie a piece of colourful yarn on the leader just above the hook or even on the shank of the hook. It's an extra attractor, but it also makes it harder for a taking fish to spit out the lure. This is a good trick whenever you feel fish are hitting short or only mouthing your lure, and you're having a hard time hooking them. Tie it so the strands of yarn hang down to about the tip of the hooks' barbs. Once a fish takes the bait the yarn fibres will often hang up on its many fine teeth, upping your chances of a good hook-set.

latched on. At the most, you'll manage a shallow hook-set that isn't going to hold a panic-stricken fish for long. It's always better to wait until you feel the fish jerk the bait a second time (some even say a third), or until the fish has taken it firmly between the jaws and starts to leave. Now it's time to dig your heels in, haul back and sink that treble in as deep as your tackle will let you.

Playing a Salmon from the Bank

Now, how to deal with a salmon once it's on. In my experience, it's much easier to keep a salmon on the line than a sea trout. Sea trout tend to run less and roll a lot more, and by such antics they're often able to lever the hook loose. Salmon also roll, but much less. They seem to be aware of the angler at the other end and are mainly intent on escape by running (or flying!) off in different directions. The only thing the angler needs to do is keep the pressure on, no matter what course the fish takes. (Obviously, if you are fishing barbless this is even more important.) By pressure I mean keeping the rod up and well bent over. As long as you've made certain beforehand that your tackle and connections are up for the fight, there's no reason why you shouldn't eventually land the fish (see box 'Tackling-up for tackle-busting salmon', p. 125).

That doesn't mean there won't be hairy moments. For one thing, salmon have the unnerving habit of head-shaking. At least once during the fight, usually soon after latching on, they will stop dead and violently shake the lure. Don't worry; do nothing, just keep the pressure on. Looking for this characteristic move, and whether your fish is running or rolling, will usually give you an early indication of whether you're into a salmon or a big sea trout.

Salmon also like to jump, even more than sea trout do. If they do, what then? Old-school fly-fishers used to say drop your rod tip, so the fish can't break the leader when it's falling. Forget that! You've got good strong line; all you need to care about is not letting it go slack!

Experts agree that when playing a salmon you've got to take charge – 'let it know who's boss'. It's good advice. One way is keeping the pressure on with a well bent rod. Another is not letting a fish stall and 'catch its breath'. If it's dug down into deep water and seems to be holding onto the bottom, lean back slowly on the rod, then reel in as you drop it back down. It's called *pumping*. Repeat this until your fish is moving again.

In fact, it's always a good policy to pump a fish in, rather than reeling continuously against its full force. The uneven pressure seems to tire it more quickly, and also saves the gears on your reel. Another power-move is *walking a fish down*. Wait until it's listing but still too frisky to land. Then, holding your rod out at right angles to the flow, walk slowly but steadily upriver. Walking it is a good way to sap the last of a fish's energy before trying to land it.

Setting the reel drag

No matter how you fish, learning to adjust your reel's drag will make hooking and playing a salmon easier and safer. If it's adjusted correctly you'll be able to set the hook good and hard, and keep enough pressure on a fighting fish to wear it down without having to worry about snapping the leader.

There are a couple ways to do this. The simplest is the jerk-and-see technique Hugh Falkus describes in *Salmon Fishing*: 'put the bait-treble in a loop of string tied to a gate-post or some other fixture. Then, standing a dozen or so yards away, tighten the line on your fixed-spool [or multiplier] reel and jerk it with the rod as hard as you can. The object of this is to set the drag adjustment on the spool so that reasonable pressure can be exerted without the clutch slipping and releasing line too easily, and also without the leader snapping however hard you jerk' (p. 337). That's OK, but it doesn't tell you how much leeway you have before something gives. Here's a better method, also simple. Start out by tightening down your drag all the way. Now hook up to something solid and jerk away. But this time, pull until something snaps. If your tackle is put together the way it should be, it will be the leader

---

that gives. Now, loosen the drag just a little, maybe half a turn to one full turn. Try to break the leader again. If it breaks, loosen the drag further. Do this until you can just pull line off the reel, but still under good force.

Many anglers set the drag once and leave it. It's simple, and, as long as you've set it right to begin with, there's no reason a fish should be able to break you off. But most anglers, once they've become thoroughly familiar with their tackle and have some experience of playing salmon, will want to change the drag freely even during a fight. This way you can do things like let a fish run off some steam before wrestling it in, or set the drag on a trolling reel when it's in a holder so a fish can take line before you tighten down and set the hook.

Most fish will take several runs. Usually one will be straight down river, hell-bent for the sea. Don't try to stop it. Let the fish take all the line it needs. If your drag is set right, it will rarely strip even 100 yd (90 m) off before turning back upstream. When it does, get ready for another hairy moment: *the rush.* A freshly hooked salmon can come upstream at great speed even against a strong current. If you happen to be wading, it might be straight at you. Don't panic, and don't let that line go limp! Fast reeling is in order, and here's where a reel with a 5:1 or 6:1 gear ratio earns its keep.

Sometimes, this early up-current run will bring the fish close to shore. Don't be fooled; it's still to 'hot' to land. Let it run past you, keeping your rod well flexed. If you can play it out the rest of the way from the downstream side, that's good. It's a better angle for keeping that hook well set in the jaw.

A fish will normally make several more runs, but each will be shorter. When it gets tired it will start to list to one side; you'll see the flash of its flanks. Now you can start manoeuvring yourself and the fish for a landing. If you're wading, start walking back to shore, and slowly up the bank a few paces, to keep a long line on the fish. Hopefully, you will already have spotted a place along the shore where you think you can land it. If it's further upstream try walking your fish to the landing site. If it's in fairly fast water try to walk it slowly into slacker water. It's easier to land a fish in slacker currents – and the slower water will supply less oxygen, so it will weaken faster.

Landing a Salmon from the Bank

You've got essentially three options: netting, tailing and gaffing.

NETTING

Netting is always the best way to land a fish when there is any chance you will be releasing it. You can land your prize much faster using a net, before it's completely spent, and so give it a better chance of surviving the affair (see 'Releasing fish', p. 108). On some rivers it's the only legal method.

Here are the rudiments. If you are going to net the fish yourself, walk down toward it while reeling in. Keep your rod high and well bent; don't let the line slacken. Try to stay below the fish if you can, so it doesn't see you and make a final frightened burst. Now slide the net underneath it from behind and lift it up. If a buddy is going to net it, then you should stay well back up on shore, walk slowly backwards until your fish can be netted in a couple of feet of water.

If you're looking for a good net, remember it's always better to get one that's too big than too small. You want one you can pull up around a decent-sized salmon from underneath, which means one with a mouth diameter of at least 25 in (64 cm). A long handle is also helpful when you're working off a steep bank. If you don't need compactness, stay away from telescopic or folding models; a one-piece net is much stronger and always ready for action. If you really need one you can break down, buy a good one. Rapala makes one of the best. Whichever net you choose, look for one with open netting of thin cord or plastic strands. Avoid those of soft, tightly-woven nylon mesh; they're a disaster when it comes to extracting hooks.

TAILING

Tailing is a good alternative to netting if you've found a landing site where the shore deepens gradually and is fairly even – not too rocky and free of other obstructions. Tailing sounds tricky but it's surprisingly easy. Once the fish is listing, bring it in toward the shore by walking back up the beach. Keep a fairly long line out, say 20 feet (6 m). Once the fish actually turns on its side you can draw it in further until its flank is touching bottom and its head is exposed. Now it's yours. Walk down to it, while reeling in line and keeping your rod high and well flexed. Once you're over the fish, hold your rod up high with one hand; reach down with the other; take the fish firmly by the tail wrist, and pull it safely ashore. If it's not a keeper, try to avoid hauling it out of the water or carrying it by the tail, as this can injure its spine (see below).

I like to tail a fish whenever it's feasible, because it saves me having to untangle fish and hooks from netting. But to tail a salmon safely you've got to pretty much exhaust it. So I reserve tailing for fish I'm going to keep. An alternative to tailing a salmon by hand is using a tailer. This is a kind of snare contraption with a noose at one end you loop around the tail wrist so you can lift the fish out. I've never used one and it seems unnecessary. On some waters it's also not permitted.

Use a priest

If you are going to keep a fish, kill it as soon as it's out of the water by knocking it on the head with a priest, *before* you remove the hook. Buy a good priest, or make one out of a piece of metal piping, or even hard wood.

GAFFING

Nowadays, using a gaff to land a fish is frowned upon almost everywhere and on more and more waters it's simply not allowed.

Where it is still legal, gaffing is usually reserved for large fish or situations where tailing or netting aren't feasible. A gaff is essentially
a big barbless hook on a long shank or handle that you stick into
a spent fish so you can get it ashore. If you need to use a gaff, here's
the best way. First, prepare the salmon for landing just like you
would if you were going to tail it. Once it's listed over in shallow
water, hook it with the gaff – preferably underneath the lower jaw
– and lift it ashore. Obviously, gaffing is out for any fish you think
you might be releasing.

If you are going to carry a gaff, get a strong one; make sure it's
got a thong around one end to slip your wrist through, and always
keep it sharp. Companies like Rapala and Abu make high quality
telescopic models. My own is one-piece; I made it from a length of
broom handle and a bent spike.

Falkus's tips on playing a salmon

Hugh Falkus (*Salmon Fishing*, pp.152–3) gave some useful tips
for successfully playing a salmon:

1) Keep the rod well up, around 2 o'clock
2) Keep a little downstream of the fish
3) Never let the line go slack
4) Never try to hold a fish when it runs
5) Always take your time playing a fish

Releasing fish

If you're going to release your fish, try to get it in quickly
before it's too exhausted. Land it with a net if you can. If you
are going to tail it, don't lift it up out of the water: this can
injure its spine. In either case try to keep the fish submerged
or at least wet while you remove the hook, and use needle-nose

---

pliers – it's faster. If the hook won't come out without causing major damage, cut the line as close to the hook as you can and leave it in. The chances are it will be expelled naturally. To release the fish, hold it loosely under the pectoral fins and around the tail while moving it back and forth gently through the water so oxygen is circulated through the gills. When the fish has recovered, it will swim out of your hands on its own.

Fishing From a Boat: Harling

Harling is a very old method for working river currents by boat. It's been used for centuries by fly-fishers as an alternative to bank fishing. The earliest baits used by salmon harlers were probably dead baits – minnows, prawns, even worms – arranged behind a leader-and-swivel arrangement so as to rotate when drawn or trailed through the water. As already noted, some of the first hardware baits for salmon harling were early artificial minnows like the Phantom and Devon, which were fished alongside flies.

But I wonder whether it wasn't early pike harlers who first realized the potential of trailing other spinning baits. Llewelyn's nineteenth-century description of 'dragging' for pike could just as well apply to harling for salmon (p. 235):

> Another common plan for taking pike was by means of a *drag*: this was a rough imitation of a fish, formed either of ivory, silver or polished iron, and armed with a single, though large, hook. To the tail end of this was attached a small piece of red cloth, the better to attract the fish. This *drag* was fastened, without swivels, to a strong well-leaded line, and was then trailed at some twenty or thirty paces in the *wake* of a boat, which, on these occasions, usually proceeded at a very slow rate.

Whoever first hit on it, harling did become – and still is – a favourite way to take salmon and sea trout, as well as pike, on many bigger streams and rivers. The reason is coverage. On waters too wide, deep, rapid or obstructed to permit efficient casting, a boat lets you cover many more likely places much more effectively than you ever could on foot.

Traditional harling was done with small, light wooden boats – dinghies, punts, cots, coracles, skiffs or similar craft – and involved one or two oarsmen (ghillies) who manoeuvred the boat and one or two anglers manning the rods. But nowadays most of us use small 10–15 ft (3–4.5 m) fibreglass boats fitted with light 4–5 hp outboards, along with oars. This makes it much easier to work against stronger currents, and to keep your hands free to operate one, two or even three rods; even to harl all alone.

Some dyed-in-the-wool bank anglers look askance on harling. 'Unskilled', they say; 'lazy man's fishing'. Falkus felt that 'catching salmon from a boat makes very small demands upon angling expertise. Most of the skill is in the head and hands of the boatman. Knowing the lies, he can place the angler in such a position that casting is negligible. No water sense is needed except by the man behind the oars.' (1984, p. 257). To people like me, 'them's fightin' words!' Most of us navigate our own boats and fish at the same time. And that demands skill. I'm still learning, but I can tell you, nothing is more testing than finding, covering, hooking, and landing a salmon all by yourself from a dinghy in strong currents (when I want a break from the rigours of harling, I fish on foot!). Harling is as challenging as you want it to be; it takes both boating and angling skills to make it work.

Harling also just happens to be one of the most effective ways to take salmon in big streams or rivers. It's also varied. You have just as many ways of delivering your lure as you do when bank fishing, plus a few more, and you can also fish some lures you otherwise wouldn't. Here are the basic techniques, each of which comes into its own under certain conditions.

Position Harling

This is basic harling. You use the boat to put yourself in a better position to cast to and cover some target; it's like wading, only with greater range. This is a good way to cover a river that is too wide, too deep or too overgrown to cover well on foot.

In the early days – before outboards – ghillies used any number of ploys to position their customers (one or two anglers) in relation to likely pieces of holding water. One was to 'let an angler down a pool' by means of a long rope hand-over-hand from shore, even tied to a tree or bridge. On very wide, rapid rivers like the Shannon or Tweed, the ghillie might walk the punt (and anglers) along the shoreline, even moor it midstream above good target water by tying it up to poles driven into the river bed.[40]

I've never tried these methods myself, but I can usually get into just as good a position by simply rowing or motoring out, and dropping anchor above a pool or some other piece of water I want to fish. This way it's easy enough to drift downstream from pool to pool, lie to lie, covering each target in turn from an ideal position above it, below or to the side. I can use the same tackle I do from the bank, the same lures, and all the same presentations from flatline to float.

In fact, with my boat for good positioning, there are few times when I don't have the advantage over a bank angler. One is when the water is low and clear, and I want to cover it by upstreaming a lure. I can do this better and with more stealth by wading in and fishing it from below. The other is when the water is very high and strong. It is possible to fish down a near-shore current break by drifting and anchoring at intervals – I've done it many times – but I can usually hit this current break just as well wading, and without the extra burden of manoeuvring a boat in heavy currents.

In my experience, using a boat for positioning is most useful when the water is very cold or very turbid, but still not too fast or high to make boating a worry. In water like this the most effective bait is delivered deep and slow. If you are fishing from the bank, the current is usually pulling your lure out of the current over towards the shore. That's fine when you're sweeping. But a boat lets you position yourself in the current – even when it's out of wading reach – so you can keep a lure hanging, backing down, or plunking inside that taking strip almost indefinitely. And you can fish it thoroughly by dropping down, re-anchoring, and casting at intervals.

Bottom Trolling

This is standard river trolling. It's how most harlers cover a stretch of river once the water gets cooler, say to 45–40°F (7–4.5°C). And it's how most of the salmon are taken in any season.

The key to *bottom trolling*, and the challenge, is keeping your lure fishing against the current within 1 ft (30 cm) of the bottom and as slowly as you can. I really mean slowly: it's like inching a lure home with your boat. The sudden appearance of a wobbling lure as it sidles up next to a salmon from behind seems to trigger even the coldest fish to strike. There are a couple of variations.

CONTOUR TROLLING

On the River Skellefteå in northern Sweden, Ingvar is the undisputed king of bottom trolling. His boat rarely comes in empty. When it does, I think twice about going out at all! Ingvar's *forte* is what I like to call *contour trolling*. Depending on the height of the water and the strength of the current he picks out an upriver course where he can keep his diving plug fishing tight along the bottom at a very slow ground speed – maybe 1½ mph if the water is cool, barely moving if it's colder. He mainly fishes Coton Cordell's Ripplin' Red Fin – a diving plug that he rehangs with top-class Owner trebles. If you ask him about colour and pattern he'll say it doesn't matter much – but I've noticed he takes care to repaint the stock finishes on all his shop-bought lures in either red-orange with a gold belly, or in dull silver-blue. To keep these fishing down near the bottom he uses a standard ledger rig: three-way-swivel with 1½–3 oz (40–90 g) of lead off a 6 in (15 cm) dropper line and about 6½ ft (2 m) of leader to the plug.

Like most of us, Ingvar trolls with a rod in one hand and the out-board tiller in the other. He tells me the real trick is keeping the dropper weight in contact with the bottom at all times. He does this by manoeuvring the boat only. If the weight looses touch, he steers a little one way or the other until it's tapping bottom again. This way he tends to fish along the same bottom contour all the way upriver. Once at the top of the water he wants to cover, he pulls up his tackle, turns the boat around, and throttles back down to the bottom to start another troll up. If fish were hitting on the first pass he might troll up the same contour again. But usually he picks another contour route by shortening or lengthening his line, or by changing weights. Or he might decide to troll up the same route at different speeds by adjusting throttle, line length, or dropper weight.

This is the most common method of harling on many of the bigger Scandinavian rivers: combing a stretch of target water one contour at a time. Some days we're a regular armada of boats, some in line, trolling up the same contour, others abreast following different routes.

TROLLING SEAMS

Contour trolling is always in force when the water is normal height and cold. But sometimes a slight variation is worth trying too. I call it *trolling seams*. This means what it says: instead of trolling up one contour route at a time, you look for breaks in the current – seams – and troll up these. This is much harder: it takes a lot keener water sense, and more tackle adjustments en route, so few anglers stick with it for long. But for the more experienced harler it's a much more efficient way to cover a river, especially when the water is high enough for many fish to concentrate along the current breaks. It's also a good way to work warmer flows.

Tackling-up for Bottom Trolling

Most trollers fish diving plugs – Rapala-type Kynocks/J-plugs. They're effective and hang up less often than other lures you fish off a dropper weight. But other lures are worth a try too. Devons have a good reputation as trolling plugs. Thin-blade spoons – favoured by many stillwater trollers – can also be bottom trolled upriver. But it takes some trial and error to find spoons that keep a slow wobble in the current. For warmer conditions – when you want a little more speed – conventional spinners are also worth a try.

Bottom trolling calls for the same dropper/weight set-up you use for ledger fishing from the bank, with a few adjustments. A stationary three-way swivel is used to connect line – mono or braid – to leader and dropper. You might get by with standard barrel swivels if you use low-twist lures only – diving plugs, spinners, Devons. But if you are going to be trolling spoons you'll need ball-bearing swivels to keep the line from twisting. Some trollers go another step and make high-quality three-ways by slipping three ball-bearing swivels on a single split ring. Line strengths are typically in the 25–30 lb (11–13.5 kg) range for the main line, and slightly less for the leader, which is always mono. Leader lengths can vary from 3½–6½ ft (1–2 m) depending on the lure. Diving plugs and spinners tend to run lower, so they'll fish deep off a longer leader; thin-blade spoons and Devons run higher, so a shorter leader is needed to keep them down near the bottom.

For the dropper weight, simple bomb weights run off 6–12 in (15–30 cm) of 15–20 lb (7–9 kg) mono are the norm. How much lead you'll need will depend on bottom depth and current strength so you'll have to experiment. On the big northern rivers I fish, anywhere from 1–3 oz (30–90 g) will keep you tapping bottom.

ONE OR TWO RODS?

When bottom trolling, I generally fish one rod. On some waters that's all you are allowed. But I know anglers who routinely fish two rods. They hold one and stick the second behind a rowlock; they say it doubles their chances of a take. The extra rod comes with some costs though. One is keeping a salmon on once it's hit the unmanned bait, since it takes a little longer to respond to a take. In my experience, this is often enough time for a sea trout to writhe itself loose before you can get to the rod and respond. Salmon are a little easier, and they're usually still hooked once you've grabbed the rod, but there are some things you can do to make sure. One is to keep your boat moving upstream. This will keep continuous pressure on the fish while you're changing rods. Another is to use only the very best hooks you can find – at least for the lure that's fishing unmanned. Super-sharp cone-tip hooks will sink deeper and hold longer than conventional hooks and give you the extra few seconds you need before taking over. Also, choose a main line with a little flex to it. High quality mono is the traditional first choice on many rivers, but the newer superbraids with a built-in stretch factor are even better, because they give you a more solid hook-up.

MOTORING VERSUS ROWING

Most bottom trollers power their boats with small outboards, in the 4–6 hp range. But rowing in the traditional way is possible too; I've tried it on occasion. But I find it hard to keep the dropper weight bouncing along the bottom when my hands are on the oars and my rod is leaning against a rowlock. Bottom snags are more frequent and become real headaches, especially when there is any kind of current; so do fouled hooks, even simple everyday tangles – and, of course, landing any fish I manage to hook. In fact, it's harder to manage anything when you're alone and rowing. I find using braid line does help, because I can see better what's going on at the business end. Generally, though, the hassles outweigh the rewards, so I tend to reserve harling with oars for top trolling and position casting.

Top Trolling

Once the water warms to 50–65°F (10–18°C) you'll start to see more and more fish breaking the surface, especially around sunset, when they begin to migrate. These are prime conditions for top trolling. Where bottom trolling targets deep fish, top trolling targets runners higher up. The tactic is trolling lures flatline – usually within 1 ft (30 cm) of the surface – and fairly fast. You can troll against, across or with the current. It's like high sweeping or upstreaming a lure from land, only with your harling boat.

Some trollers pull lures straight up- or down-current, but it is much more effective to cover the water in big sweeping 'S' curves – sometimes called *pulling S's*. For this you want to manoeuvre your boat – whether with or against the current – back and forth laterally across the river getting as close to the bank as you can on each turn. This not only covers the water thoroughly, it also makes the trailing lure a little more attractive than on a straight pull because it varies its path, speed, and depth: slower and a little deeper on the diagonals, higher and faster around the turns nearer the bank. If fish seem to be using a well defined seam or slot, you can follow these up instead, pulling shorter S's.

How long a line to fish depends on the water. On dead clear, calm pools and glides where the spook factor comes into play, most harlers fish at least 40–50 yd (35–45 m) of line. In stretches of choppier and/or coloured water you can go down to as little as 20 yd (18 m).

You can top troll the same baits that you use for bottom trolling, even light plugs, or Devons with or without a little in-line sinker. But in my experience heavier casting spoons are ideal – skinny spoons when you are working up-current, wider spoons when working down.

To start out, if you are fishing upstream, simply drop your lure down into the water, free up your reel and let the current drag out line. But when pulling S's down-current with a sinking lure, I've found it's best to position my boat towards one bank and make a cast across current toward the middle. This way I have time to get my boat moving downriver ahead of the current before my lure has time to sink to and possibly snag the bottom.

ONE OR TWO RODS?

It can be a little trickier to fish two rods when top trolling than when bottom trolling: it's just too easy to cross lines on the turn when you're pulling S's. If you want to try, make it easy on your-self by fishing long rods – at least 9 ft (2.7 m). Place them 'abeam' so they reach out wide from opposite sides of the boat and don't make your turns too tight. As in bottom trolling, low-stretch braid line and super-sharp hooks will help with hook-ups.

MOTORING VERSUS ROWING

An outboard makes top trolling easy. But if you want to try tradi-tional harling by oar power, top trolling offers the perfect chance. Unlike bottom trolling, it doesn't give you the added worry of dealing with bottom-snags when your hands are full of oars. It's also quieter, which some harlers feel can give you the edge over outboard-users in warm, clear, calm water, when the fish are edgy. But keep it simple and fish only one rod. When I top troll I nearly always row. I find that wrapping a little cloth or leather around the shaft of the rowlocks keeps noise down. I don't know if it's crit-ical to my hook-up rate, but it's soothing to me.

Tip: Tether your oars

Run a short line through each oar near the handle and attach it to the rowlock. That way your oars won't slip into the water when you drop them to grab the rod.

Tackling-up for Top Trolling

Your trusty flatline outfit will do for top trolling – same swivel and leader set-up, same rod and reel.

Back Trolling

Back trolling is the boater's rendition of drifting. Only, in my experience, it's much more effective, because you can keep your bait's speed down. It works almost any time, but it's most effective when the water is clear and colder than say 45°F (7°C), when fish are hugging the bottom. Back trolling is my favourite way of harling for salmon, and also for sea trout. I described it in *Spin-Fishing for Sea Trout*:

> It amounts to backing your boat down river in a zigzag pattern – just a little slower than the current – while keeping your lure drifting deeply on about 100 ft (30 m) of line. As when drifting from the bank, it's imperative that you keep your lure bouncing along the bottom, and this is easier to do with the more sensitive and responsive braid line. You will still get your share of hang-ups when back trolling. But it's much easier to free snags from a boat.
>
> Traditional back trolling calls for an angler and an oarsman. When I'm taking an angler out, I man the oars and we drift down without power. The routine is to first motor up to the head of the water we want to cover, usually trolling a spoon or plug along the way. Once at the top, we cut the motor and start our drift. I keep the bow up-current and break our speed

by dragging the oars. I also angle the prow a little one way or the other, so the boat 'slides' diagonally from bank to bank. The angler sits in the [stern], or middle, facing down-current while working the lure along the bottom just like drifting from the bank.

Now that's the ideal situation: one oarsman, one angler. But when I'm in the boat alone I have to make a few adjustments. I troll upstream as before, but when I drift down, I use the motor to control the drift. I sit in the stern with one hand on the outboard control, the other on the rod. I position myself so I'm facing sideways toward the bank. This way I can keep a better sense of drift speed and also my boat's course. It's pretty easy to weave the boat from bank to bank in a gentle down-current zigzag using the motor's rudder. It is harder to keep your lure bouncing ideally along the bottom with one hand while controlling the drift of the boat with the other. It's a matter of co-ordination. But you can get surprisingly good at it with practice.

Unlike trolling up-current, I use one rod when drifting downstream. It's hard enough to pull off a good drift with one set up, impossible with two.

This is classic harling. Since the nineteenth century it's been closely associated with the River Tay, although it was common on other big rivers too, like the Moy, Spey and Shannon. In south Wales anglers followed their own unique traditions of back trolling from tiny skin- or fabric-covered wickerwork boats called coracles. They could still be seen on rivers like the Dee, Severn, Cleddau, Usk, Nyfer (Nevern), Wye and Llwchwr (Loughor) in the early twentieth century, and I gather from reading the web pages of the Welsh Coracle Society (see www.welsh-coracles.co.uk) that there has been something of a rebirth of this old angling tradition. It warms my heart!

Tackling-up for Back Trolling

I like back trolling, because I can use the same outfit I use for flatlining.

Give bank anglers a break

Harling can take up a lot of space on the river. Your boat and line can easily interfere with anglers working from the bank. Code of the river: bank fishermen have the right of way.

Tip: Under tough conditions, keep it simple

When harling alone in heavy water or in a stiff wind, fish one rod and keep your tackle set-up simple. Playing and landing a fish with one hand while manoeuvring the boat with the other is challenging enough in easy water; it's much harder in a strong current or when the wind is fighting you. Even a tangled line becomes a big problem then. So save the second rod for easier conditions. Do the same when you are rowing alone: keep it simple.

Drift Jigging

When I want to try standard deep jigging I wait until I'm in my boat. It's much easier to keep the lure fishing vertically in a nice controlled way, and there is much less risk of foul-hooking fish. This is one of the most effective ways to fish down a seam or slot where fish are running. It works anytime but seems to be most effective when the water is over 45°F (7°C).

Drift jigging is a lot like back trolling, only now you want to fish your lure more or less vertically under the boat in a controlled sink-and-draw. The best lure for the job is a jigging spoon – something like a Crippled Herring, Swedish Pimple, homemade Fattail or a reversed skinny spoon.

Start by rowing or motoring to the top of the stretch of water you want to cover, put the outboard into neutral (or, if you are rowing, stow the oars) and start your drift down-current. Drop your lure straight down over the side until it hits the bottom. Now lift it up fairly fast about 2 ft (60 cm), then drop it back down more slowly. Don't let it fall freely: you want to follow it down with the rod tip so it stays more or less vertical and wiggles down on the drop. Otherwise, it falls too erratically and risks foul-hooking a fish. Remember, salmon almost always hit a jigging lure on the drop, so be ready.

In drift jigging, matching lure weight to drift speed is important. You'll need to try several baits, but on bigger rivers you'll probably fish something in the 1–3 oz (30–85 g) range in order to stay fishing vertically. If you find your lure and line starting to trail behind the boat, try slowing your drift speed by engaging the outboard, dropping a drift anchor[41] or tying on a heavier lure. Jigging near bottom is the norm, but you can also make several passes and cover the same stretches at different depths.

Tackling-up for Drift Jigging

About 2–6 ft (0.5–2 m) of mono leader in the 30–40 lb (13.5–18 kg) range is usually run off a good ball-bearing swivel tied to the main line. But anglers differ on the best main lines for drift jigging. Some prefer mono, because it keeps steady tension on the spoon for a more controlled drop. Others like the thinner no-stretch braid because it's more sensitive to takes and lets you get down with less weight. For reels, multipliers by Abu, Shimano and Daiwa are favourites.

Hooking, Playing and Landing Fish from a Boat

Too many boat anglers lose salmon unnecessarily. The main reason is panic. Fishing on foot there's not much else you need to focus on but hooking, playing and getting your fish to land. In a boat there are many more, like manoeuvring the boat in the current, dealing with a motor, or an anchor, or the oars, or maybe more than one rod. The natural reaction is to rush, and that's a mistake. One of the things that separates experienced harlers from the rest is their calm and measured response to a fish on the line. How best to manage all this is going to depend on just how you're fishing, in what kind of water, whether you are rowing or motoring, and whether you're alone or have some help. But, whatever the situation, taking things slowly is the key to success.

Hooking a Salmon from a Boat

If you're fishing while at anchor with the rod in hand, responding to a strike is no different than when you are fishing on foot. If you're trolling in a moving boat, other factors come into play. When back trolling or drift jigging – whether your rod is in your hand or sitting in a holder – be ready for gentle takes and wait for the fish to make a solid move first before striking.

Trolling up- or down-current is a little different again. It's normal to set the drag on the rod you're holding just as you would for bank fishing – pretty tight. The motion of the boat alone is usually enough to set the hook firmly, especially when fishing with a low-stretch braid line. If you are fishing stretchier mono, it doesn't hurt to make sure by giving the rod a good hard yank.

For unmanned rods carrying braid line it's more common to set the drag looser than normal. This guards against getting broken by a hard striker, besides giving you time to grab the rod and take control while the fish takes line. The looser drag isn't necessary with mono, due to the greater play you get from the stretchier line.

In any event, it's important to clear things up on deck *before* playing and landing your fish. Reel in any other lines, get the oars up, pull the anchor in and stow it out of the way. The landing net can cause all kinds of grief at the wrong moment, so make sure you've placed it somewhere you can get at it, and not where you'd have to dig through a bunch of gear to free it. I like to lay the net flat along the seats with the mesh end toward the bow and the handle within easy reach.

If you're not alone, responding to a fish on the line is fairly easy. One of you grabs the live rod with the fish, the other clears up. If you are alone, though, it's a little trickier. Above all, stay calm and measured. Pick up the live rod first, and make sure you've got a solid hook-set by clamping your thumb down on the spool of the reel and giving a few hard yanks. Then put the live rod down – either in a holder or behind a rowlock. Now you can clear things away. Even if you don't rush, this shouldn't take more than 20–30 seconds. Now, take up the live rod again, screw down the drag if it's loose, and go to work. Some dispense with the hook-up check altogether and clean up first. Most of the time the salmon is still on when they take up the live rod.

No matter how well you do all this, you're going to lose more fish on the unmanned rod than on the one you're holding. Some anglers feel the greater number of takes fishing two rods outweighs the higher loss rate and the added handling costs. Others don't, and so fish one rod. Your choice!

Playing a Salmon from a Boat

In my experience, it's usually easier to play a salmon from a boat than from shore. You can manoeuvre more freely, and you've got the option of using the motor or even oars to keep pressure on the fish. But this assumes you've got a good, solid hook-set and readied the boat as described above.

I'm familiar with two approaches to playing a fish. One is to cut the motor, or pull the oars in, as soon as a fish is on, and then let the boat drift freely while it's being played and landed; if there are no rapids and few obstructions to worry about, this works. The only drawback is you can end up well downriver, and other boats need to get out of your way. I've watched some boats drift for nearly 1 mi (1.6 km) before getting a big fish into the boat.

But most harlers – myself included – like to maintain power and play the fish *with the boat* so to speak. This amounts to manoeuvring so you keep continuous pressure on the fish. If it's downstream, you hold station against the current. If it rushes further down, you back down with it while keeping the pressure on. When it comes back upstream, you move upstream, and so on. This way you might play a fish for several minutes without reeling in at all. But don't keep this up until the fish is completely spent: a fish that can't swim against the current becomes a 'dead' weight adrift in the river and very hard to get into the boat. Instead, once you feel it tiring, cut the power and let yourself drift toward the fish as you are pumping it in.

Now, this is easy to do using the outboard motor – one hand on the motor, one on the rod. But I've also pulled it off with oars where the current isn't too strong – where it is, I simply pull up the oars and play the fish as I drift downstream.

There can be variations on this, of course, depending on circumstances. For example, a fish that takes a lure well upstream when you're trolling down-current can pose a challenge. Eventually, it will make a downstream run. It can be hard to keep pressure on if you are drifting, and most anglers don't want to throttle up fast enough to stay ahead, especially with other boats and bank anglers around. The best move seems to be to pull the boat over towards one bank until the fish passes downstream then pull back out into midstream. Some anglers even beach their boat and play the fish on foot. With some experience, making the right decisions will become second nature.

Landing a Salmon from a Boat

A landing net is really the only sensible option for landing salmon from a boat. I've seen people hanging over the side to gaff a fish, but it's risky. What you want is a good, strong, long-handled net. It could be the same one you use from the shore if the handle is long enough, say around 6 ft (1.8 m). In any case, you want it with an opening at least a 24 in (62 cm) in diameter, and if possible netting of open, thin cord or plastic strands, so you can free treble hooks more easily.

Just as when playing a fish from land the key to getting a salmon in the net is not trying to get it in too soon. Make sure your fish is tired and under control before you slide the net underneath and lift it up around it. If you're alone, keep your rod up high with one hand and slide the net under with the other. But stay seated or on your knees – don't stand up, unless you're looking to take a bath! If you've got help, this is all much easier. You can even stand up if all seems steady enough; keep the rod high and let your partner do the netting.

PROBLEM SCENARIOS

Netting a salmon from a boat shouldn't be a problem as long as you can avoid two potentially disastrous scenarios.

The first of these is snagging a hook on the outside of the netting (fishing a plug with two or three trebles hanging off it makes this a very real risk). The best ways to avoid it are: first, never to swipe at a fish that's thrashing around, but wait for it to tire before sliding the net underneath; and second, to use a really big net – big enough that you don't have to try to slide a fish in head or tail first, but instead lift the net up around the whole length of the fish.

Still, sooner or later – if you are lucky – you'll hook a fish that's too big for your net to take in all at once. The old fly-fisher's saw says a big fish ought to go in head first. That's fine if all the hooks are inside the fish's jaw – if there are any hanging outside it's a recipe for disaster. Instead, try to get the fish's head up high, and then slide the net up around it from the tail. This isn't perfect, but there's less risk of a fatal netting snag than when trying to net it head first.

If all this fails and you end up with a fish hooked to the outside of the netting, you've got a couple of options, short of gaffing it. You can try quickly turning or flipping the net inside out and hopefully end up with the fish still snagged, but on the inside. This is not impossible, at least with smaller salmon – I've managed it on occasion. The other (which I'll admit rarely works) is hauling the fish into the boat by the netting. Good luck!

The second potential disaster is a fish that's run under the boat. The best way to avoid this is by keeping the fish at a safe distance to begin with, until it's weak enough to be controlled by manoeuvring the boat (as described above). If you can't, and the fish is rushing toward you, the best route is quickly to pull up everything that's not already up – oars, anchor line, even outboard – so fish and line can pass under the boat without hindrance. As long as there's nothing under the boat for the line to catch on it's no big deal if the fish runs underneath – and even out the other side (just move around the boat until you're on the same side as the fish again). If your fish does manage to get under you and wrapped around something, you're probably going to lose it. As a last-ditch effort you could try beaching your boat. If you're lucky the salmon might still be there and close enough for you to net or tail it.

Use braid when rowing

When harling by oar power, watching the rod tip is your only means of keeping track of a lure's action, and whether or not it's got fouled with debris. This is much easier to do with the more sensitive braid line. Braid also makes rowing easier: it's much thinner than mono of the same strength, so there's less water resistance. But remember to set the reel's drag a little looser than you would with mono.

Tackling-up for tackle-busting salmon

You can get away with less than perfect tackle connections with sea trout, but not with salmon. Salmon are notorious for escaping by snapping, bending, pulling loose and stripping tackle and connections. Take nothing for granted. Make sure everything, from hook to reel, is strong, in good working order and well connected. And don't ask the fish to do it! Check things out *before* you get your line wet. Sink the hook into a board or a tree branch and yank away at it until you're satisfied a salmon can't break you off. Getting a salmon on the hook is hard enough; don't end it in despair because you overlooked some link in the tackle chain.

Tying Things Together: Knots

You only need to know a few knots, if they're the right ones. Here they are:

Loop or Rapala Knot

This is the knot for attaching spoons or diving plugs to the leader so you don't cramp their action. It's very easy to tie, and strong. Remember to make four turns before you bring it back through the eye.

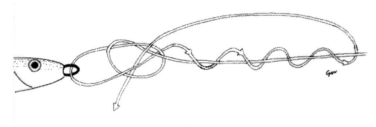

Loop or Rapala knot

Trilene Knot

This is the best knot for tying mono to a swivel or a sinker or to any lure you aren't worried about dampening the action of, like a spinner. It's strong and easy to tie – even in a rocking boat. It's the only one I use. But a decent alternative is the more traditional *Tucked Half-Blood* or *Clinch* knot. Make four turns on each.

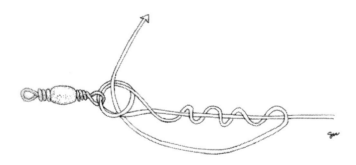

Trilene knot

Double-Tucked Half-Blood and Double Trilene Knots

Braids are more slippery than mono. Tie them the same, and you risk them pulling loose. The best way to keep knots in these lines tight is to tie them wet with either a *Double-Tucked Half-Blood* or *Double Trilene* knot. I use the Double Trilene, because you end up with four loops through the eye which makes the knot more abrasion-resistant.

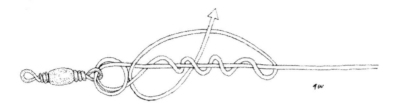

Double-tucked Half Blood knot

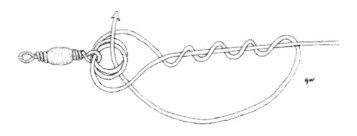

Double Trilene knot

Double Grinner Knot

If you have to splice two lines together (not recommended), the best way to do it is with a *Double Grinner*. It's stronger than the Blood Knot but harder to tie. Think of it as two knots, and then tie each separately. Make four turns on each.

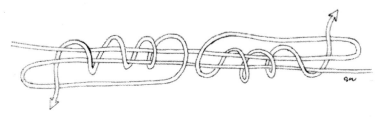

Double Grinner knot

Mono Reel Knot

This is the final link between you and the fish, so make it a good one. For tying monofilament directly to the spool use the *Mono Reel* knot which has a knotted free end to prevent slippage. Make four turns on the main part. Braids are prone to slide around the spool if tied directly to it. So if you are using braid for the main line, tie it first to a few feet of mono by a *Double Grinner* knot. Then attach the mono to the spool with the *Mono Reel* knot.

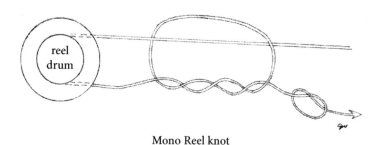

Mono Reel knot

Bobber-stop Knot

This knot keeps a running bobber from sliding too far up the line, but still clears the rod guides so you can reel all the way in. It's basically a Surgeon's knot made with about five inches of nylon No. 15–30 Dacron of about the same diameter as your line. Take two or three turns around the line first, then the same in the loop, and pull the coils tight.

An angler uses his boat to give himself a better position for covering prime holding water around the bridge pilings

Ingvar's boat rarely comes in empty

Trolling up a break or seam in the current is one of the most
efficient ways to cover fish, especially in higher water conditions

A harler pulling S's up a gentle glide by oar-power

A lone harler plays a salmon mid-river. He keeps the motor engaged to hold the boat's position and help keep pressure on the fish

A couple of nice fish taken on a pearl and red-orange Mobacken spoon

Back home late with a 16 lb (7 kg) autumn
fish taken at sunset on a Fattail spoon

A 1⅜ oz (40 g) Abu Koster spoon fitted out with a fluorescent orange, white
and black tiger pattern ready for high-water duty

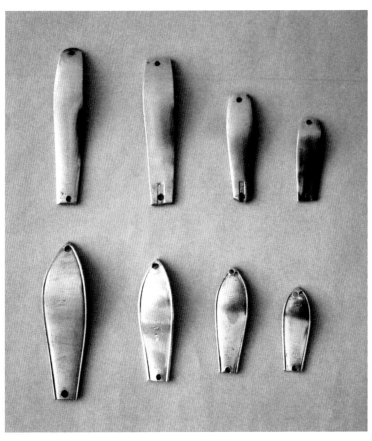

Spoon bodies made from the handles of table spoons and forks

A Fathead jigging spoon ready for action

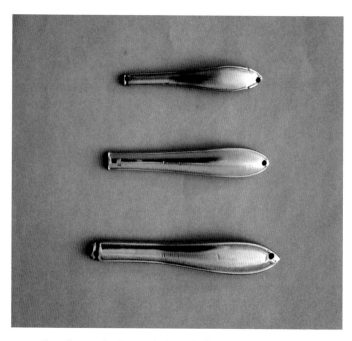

Fattail spoon bodies made from the handles of table knives

Wide-body Mobacken spoon bodies made from soft lead or tungsten
(shown front and back)

Thin-blade spoon bodies made from tin-can metal

Home-made wooden minnows with mounts

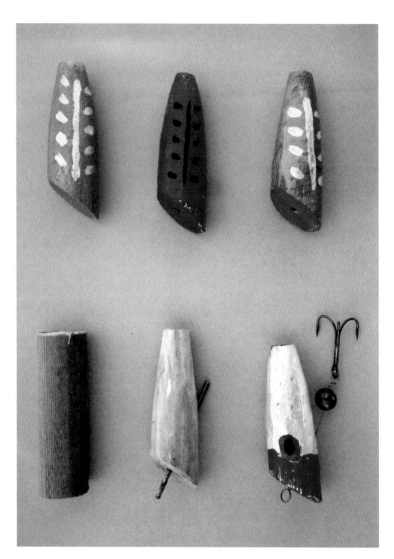

Home-made wooden J-plugs

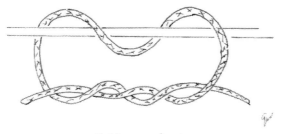

Bobber-stop knot

Monofilament or Braid Line?

A few years ago it was easy to argue for the virtues of mono – whether nylon or fluorocarbon – over the newer braid line. Braid was too brittle and too prone to fraying and weakening; it floated, making deep-sweeping more difficult than with sinking mono; it had no flex, so it was difficult to keep pressure on a fish, and a hard-hitting fish could snap it on a troll; it didn't work well in freezing temperatures because it carried too much water into the reel. Now all that has changed. New, improved hi-tech braids, often called superbraids or spectra lines, are much tougher, have some built-in flex and come in sinking varieties. Some are even designed for ice-water fishing. In fact, it's hard to think of reasons not to use new braid line for nearly all kinds of river fishing.

Superbraid's much greater sensitivity is probably its greatest advantage. With braid you can keep track of your lure's action more easily by watching the rod tip or feeling it in your hands. This makes fishing tight to a snaggy bottom much easier and much cheaper (in terms of snagged and lost hardware). It also helps your reaction time at the take by translating the hook set instantly, and, because it has less stretch, you can drive a hook deeper into a salmon's hard mouth more easily. Braid is also much stronger for its diameter than mono, so you can pack more on the reel (plenty of room for those oversized salmon that like to run long), and you can cast lighter lures much further. Braid also trolls more easily, because of reduced water resistance on the thinner line, and allows you to keep a light lure or lure/sinker combination fishing deeper than it would on mono of the same breaking strain. For example, the diameter of a 65 lb (30 kg) superbraid is about that of 15 lb (7 kg) mono.

Arguably the only drawbacks to today's braids are that they are much more tangle-prone than mono, that they still tend to ice up,[42] and that they're much pricier: two or three times as much as mono.

Choosing the Right Rod and Reel

It's common to think about rod and reel before anything else. You buy an outfit you like the look of, or have heard about, or you use one that's given you good service with trout or pike. You might end up with a sweet match for salmon too – or you might not. Years back, I launched my salmon-spinning career with a lightweight sea trout outfit. No problems, at first. Then a big fish stripped the gears clean on the fixed-spool reel. Not long after that I snapped the rod in half throwing out a heavy dropper weight.

Basic Considerations

A better approach to choosing the right rod and reel is to think about the combination or combinations that would be best for the kinds of rivers you'll be fishing and the ways you'll be fishing them. Ask yourself some questions. Is the river big and deep, or small and shallow? Will I be fishing mainly from the bank or from a harling boat? Will I need to cast long, or from cramped overgrown quarters? Do I want to fish mostly flatline? With ledgers? Floats? How much terminal weight do I want to cast? Up to 1 oz (30 g)? 1½ oz (40 g)? More? Will I be trolling with lighter terminal gear or fishing deep with heavier set-ups? Also, will I be fishing mainly non- or low-stretch braid lines or more flexible mono? Finally, how many rods and reels do I want? One, two, or more? Making the right choices at this stage can mean the difference between efficient, effective and enjoyable fishing, and something less (not to speak of saving versus wasting money!). You might ask a more experienced spinner what they'd recommend, or ask the pros at the tackle shop.

Rod

As a general guideline, think about a rod in terms of its power rating first. This is how much terminal weight it's designed to handle. It should be marked right on the rod above the reel mount. If it says 'lure wt. ½ to 1½ oz' you know it can handle terminal loads – lure and/or lure-plus-sinker weights – of up to 1½ oz (42.5 g) without over-flexing and possibly breaking. A rod with that rating or higher will have no trouble handling a salmon. Next, think about length. Longer rods let you cast further, keep more line out of the water, and hang a lure further out from the shore. But they require more room. Shorter rods are easier to use when you've got limited space – say, along a wooded stream bank or in a small boat – but they won't throw a lure as far as a longer rod. Flex is also a consideration. If you are going to fish mainly monofilament, think about a rod with a fairly stiff action. This will compensate for monofilament's relative insensitivity, enhance feel and improve lure control. If you are going to fish mainly non- or low-stretch braid, think about a softer-action rod. It will lend your tackle a little more give when a fish hits, and make it easier to keep constant pressure on a fighting fish.

Reel

For the reel, the basic question becomes multiplier or fixed-spool. It used to be that salmon spinners fished multipliers whenever they could afford to, because they were stronger, had much better drag systems and were easier to feed line with than fixed-spool reels. But modern fixed-spools with bait-runner or free-line functions can match multipliers on most points, and usually at half the price. They also cast a light bait much more easily than a multiplier can, especially from cramped spaces. And you can carry several spools loaded with different lines and change them quickly at the waterside. Multipliers still get the nod for strength and endurance, though, so they are probably the better choice for ledgering, for trolling with heavy terminal tackle and for some high-impact presentations like ripping.

Whichever kind of reel you decide on, choose one with quality and simplicity in mind. More ball-bearings are always better than fewer; so is a gear ratio of at least 5:1. Look for a good drag system and, if it's a fixed-spool reel, a bait-runner/free-line function. To ensure overall quality stay with the best brands, like Shimano, Daiwa, Okuma and Abu Garcia.

Some Recommendations

If you like it simple, then a medium- to heavy-action rod of 9 or 9½ ft (2.7 or 2.9 m), rated for 1½–1¾ oz (40–50 g) weights, used with a heavy-duty fixed-spool reel with a bait-runner/free-line function is hard to beat. It will cope with just about all your flatlining needs in style, besides being serviceable for lighter ledger and float fishing, as well as trolling.

My current standard flatline rod is a 9 ft (2.7 m) medium/stiff-action Shimano Catana with a 1½ oz (40 g) weight rating. My reel is a sturdy Shimano 4000 series with twin handles for fast pickup, reverse-slip brake, easily accessible quick-action rear drag and interchangeable spools. This is the same outfit I use for sea trout, and it's taken salmon of over 20 lb (9 kg) with no signs of trouble. For line changes, I use two spools, one loaded with floating braid, the other with sinking braid or mono. On days when I'll be fishing both high and low, I carry both spools and change between the two at will.

I've got nothing against multipliers – most of my colleagues use them – but they need lots of room to cast. A fixed-spool reel lets me reach more lies than my multiplier-using buddies, like those nice near-shore current seams tucked along densely wooded banks. The only time I fish a multiplier – outside my boat – is when I'm going to be doing a lot of ripping. Continuous ripping puts a strain on the bail arm of a fixed-spool reel, especially one loaded with low-stretch braid. So if I intend ripping for more than a few hours I screw on my multiplier.

Now I don't do too much float fishing. When I do, I simply add a float to my normal flatline outfit. If I did more of it, I'd think about a longer rod. Avid float fishers prefer rods of 10–12 ft (3–3.5 m), or even longer, for the same reasons worm anglers do: it's easier to keep your rig fishing out from the bank where you can't wade; it's easier to keep a straight line because there's less in the water and less drag; it's easier to mend line when you need to.

Same goes for plunking or heavy ledger fishing. For me, it's the exception rather than the norm. The little I do, I do with my trusty flatline outfit. I've even tossed dropper weights much heavier than my rod is rated for with no problems – so far. If I plunked more regularly, I'd get a longer, heavier-action rod – something 9½–12 ft (3–3.5 m) long – rated for dealing with terminal loads up to say 8 oz (225 g) and fitted with a good strong multiplier. I'd think about a rod-holder too. According to Canadian guide Steve Kaye, 'a good heavy-duty rod-holder is also a must, as more than just a few rods have been dragged into the river by large fish, the old tree branch will not cut it here'. A common do-it-yourself solution is a 4–5 ft (1.2–1.5 m) piece of metal pipe you drive into the shore.

As I said, you can get away with your flatline outfit for most harling too. If you're going to be using your boat mainly to position yourself better for casting, that's clearly your best choice. But most anglers who spend a lot of time trolling have a second rod and reel for that. A medium-action rod of 8½–9½ ft (2.6–2.9 m) fitted with a multiplier is a common solution. The shorter rod is a little easier to handle in a small boat, and it's easier to work the clutch on a multiplier with one hand while keeping the other on the outboard tiller. My harling combo is a 7½ ft (2.3 m) rod with a long, stiff butt and a soft tip. It's a nice match for the braid I usually fish. My reel is the simple, strong and reliable Abu Ambassadeur 5000 multiplier.

Use mono backing with braid mainline

Modern superlines like braid are expensive. Why pay for filling the reel with it when you aren't going to be actively using more than 100 yd (90 m)? Better to buy what you need and back it up with cheaper monofilament. Here's how.

On one spool, wind on 100 yd (90 m) of superline. Connect it to mono of about 20–30 lb (9–14 kg) breaking strain, using a Double Grinner knot. Wind the mono on until you've filled the spool – to about ⅛–¼ in (3–6 mm) below the lip. On a second spool, connect the ends of the mono with a reel knot, and wind both lines on. Mono backing is also better because it retains less moisture deep on the spool.

Wading and Waders

You don't have to fish the fly to wear waders. There are several advantages for the spinner too. The first is better positioning. When all is said and done, success with salmon is mainly a matter of covering plenty of fish. Being able to wade out into the flow lets you position yourself so you can cover a lie effectively with your cast. It gets you clear of vegetation or other obstructions along the bank. It also lets you hang, back down or plunk a lure from straight upstream – all good moves when the water is high and coloured or very cold, for example.

Another advantage of wading is accessibility. There are heavily wooded streams and rivers where the only easy way to reach a nice pool or run is via the shallow margins. Waders let you do that, even if you decide to cover the target from shore once you're there. Stealth is another advantage. It might not seem obvious, but it's usually much easier to stay low and out of a salmon's sight standing up to your waist in water than standing high and dry on the shore. Due to the reflection and refraction of light on the water, it's actually hard for a fish to see much above the surface except inside a window of about 45° straight overhead. Outside that zone, especially in bright sunlight or moonlight, it's like looking into a mirror, because, viewed from below, the surface of the water is reflective. Obviously if you are fishing clear, low water it's best to stay outside that window. You can do that by wading deep.

As for choosing among the different types of waders available, it depends on how you're going to use them and in what season. If you're mainly looking for better positioning, and accessibility along larger streams and rivers, then the trusty old PVC/rubber thigh waders will probably do. They're simple, fairly light, easy to get on and off and don't cost an arm and a leg. For a little more money you can get these in lighter, high-tech polymer membranes such as Aquatex or Aquavent. These are all meant for warmer conditions. But if you get them big enough you can pull them over a pair of warm trousers.

If you want to be able to wade deeper – up to your waist or even chest – choosing the best waders gets a bit more complicated. First, PVC is usually not an option. Your choices now are between waders made from polymer membranes and those made from thicker (about 4 mm) neoprene. If you are going to be fishing water from 30–40°F (-1–7°C) you'll want the neoprene for warmth. Waders in both materials can come in two-piece outfits, where the boots (and socks) are separate, or one-piece with boots attached. All are much more expensive than the PVC hip waders. Your choice.

4. Tactical Guide

A Tactical Approach

We now have a range of presentations for covering fish in all sorts of flows, plus a range of lures with which to get a strike out of any salmon we cover. The final ingredient for success is determining where and when to best utilize these assets. This calls for tactical thinking: learning to read the water and the weather so you can locate the most likely salmon lies and assess the lures and presentations that will give you your best chance of action in the given conditions.

Know the regulations

There are very few, if any, rivers where you can simply buy a permit and fish when and how you want. Besides legal taking seasons and bag limits, most rivers (and even specific beats) carry restrictions on spinning. On some it's allowed only on certain sections of water, or only after you've given fly-fishing a try, or only in high water conditions, or between certain dates. On some waters spinning is forbidden altogether. And on some waters certain presentations are forbidden or discouraged, like upstreaming or jigging. There may be restrictions or bans on lures with more than one treble, double

---

or even single hook, or on using barbed hooks altogether, on tipping lures with dead baits or scents, or using lead shot of a certain size/weight. Many waters also forbid the use of gaffs or tailers, and either strongly encourage or require you to release all or some of your catch. Many waters also restrict the use of harling boats, with or without motors, or may require you to fish with a ghillie. Obviously you need to know the regulations governing any waters you plan to fish before you set out. Happily it's pretty easy to do this nowadays via the Internet, since many of the more popular salmon rivers have their own Web pages, where you can also get up-to-date information on water conditions, tackle recommendations, recent catches, ghillies and boats for hire, accommodation, etc., along with the local codes.

Reading the Conditions

Before you get your lure wet, ask yourself the following questions about the conditions you'll be fishing in.

Where are the Fish?

That's the main question. The first thing to do is take a good look at the water. Even on a small river most of the water is empty of fish most of the time. You've got to work out which bits salmon are likely to be in and when, so that all your lures and presentations don't go to waste. Like most anglers, I try to think of any stretch of water in terms of the parts and features that are more or less useful to salmon (and so valuable to me) under different circumstances.

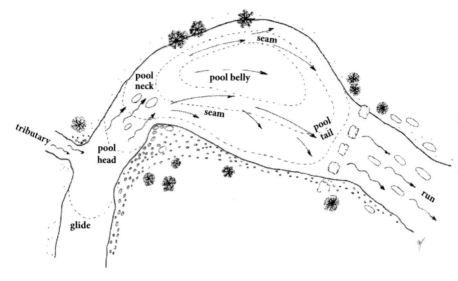

Salmon tend to use different sections of a river at different times. So knowing the sections to target requires knowledge of both the water and prevailing conditions. For example, pool tails fish best at dawn, dusk or when it's cloudy; runs when it's warm and sunny; water below tributaries when it's very warm or very cold; pool bellies when it's near freezing or at dawn when it's very warm. Glides, pool necks and heads, breaks (seams) or pockets in the current, and water near cover are always worth some attention.

The Pool Neck and Head

In general, salmon prefer water flows of moderate strength with a broken surface and enough depth so they don't feel exposed. That's why the neck and head of a pool are often some of the most productive pieces of water you can fish. This is where the faster, broken water from the run above slows down as it passes into the top of a pool. Depth is usually from 6–12 ft (1.8–3.6 m). But the surface is more important. To be good holding water it's got to have enough ripple or chop on the surface to provide secure cover. This is a prime spot for salmon. It almost always contains some fish, and, because of the arousal involved in competing for lies, these fish are often aggressive and ready takers.

The Glide

Some rivers, especially in their lower reaches, develop long pieces of pretty featureless water called glides. Look for stretches with good depth, a choppy surface and/or lots of cover along the banks. Fish will use these like they do a pool neck, so this can be prime water that fishes well under most conditions.

The Pool Belly

The very belly or middle section of a pool where the water is deepest and the current weakest is usually empty of fish. But there are a couple of exceptions. The first is during very warm weather at night, in the wee, pre-dawn hours. If temperatures have dropped overnight, fish may sit in the deepest, calmest part of the pool, where cooler water has accumulated. Not usually for long, though: once the sun hits the water they move up higher into the security of the broken water towards the head. Another time to find salmon in the belly is when the water is near freezing. Then the deeper water is actually a bit warmer than it is higher up – ice floats, remember![43] – and fish may migrate to these slightly warmer lies.

Sonar fish finders

Most rivers aren't deep enough to make sonar fish finders worthwhile. But if you are near the mouth fishing channels over 20 ft (6 m) deep, a fish finder can really help. Besides letting you find fish, it also locates bottom features, gives you depth and even water temperature readings. In short, it lets you target your trolling. One tactic is to guide your boat slowly either up or down trailing a lure in a big S-pattern. Once a fish shows on the screen, you adapt the boat's course, making adjustments in lure or dropper weights, line length or boat speed, so you cover your target. Talk about efficiency!

The Pool Tail

The tail of a pool is where the current slows and gets shallower just before it breaks into the next run. This is classic target water for low-light fishing – either dusk to dawn, or when it's cloudy or overcast. That's because salmon typically rest here after pushing up through the faster water below.

The Run

This is where the water bounces over exposed or barely submerged rocks. It might be at the end of rapids, or where the water enters a pool (head-in or run-in) or leaves it (run-out), and it may be only 2 ft (60 cm) deep. Runs provide cover and highly oxygenated and somewhat cooler water during the warmest seasons. So this is where to look for takers on a bright hot summer's day.

The Current Break or Seam

They might not always act like it, but salmon are basically energy savers. That means they almost always take the easiest way up through fast or heavy water. Favourite routes are just along the outer edges of the main current where faster water meets slower, called the current break, slot, crease or seam. Find these, and you're on the path to finding active fish. (Falkus called them taking strips.) But seams change. When the water is very high they might be very close to the shore and 1 ft (30 cm) or less wide. When it's low they can spread across much of the stream. Foam lines sometimes form right long these breaks so keep an eye out for them.

Pockets

Almost anywhere the current is obstructed, and hence a pocket of weaker current forms, is a potential lie. Salmon use these pockets as temporary resting spots when pushing up through fast water or as longer term lies. Boulders, depressions, holes, sunken logs, pilings, etc. are all worth targeting. Learn where they are when the water is low, so you can still find them when it's high.

Tip: Where salmon lie

Salmon don't usually lie directly behind obstructions like boulders. Instead look for them right in front, to either side, right on top, or further back where the broken current comes together again.

Cover

Salmon don't like to feel exposed. Anything that supplies cover will potentially hide fish. Overhanging bushes, branches, fallen trees, roots, bridge pilings, piers, undercut banks, accumulations of flotsam, even ice build-up along the bank – all are worth investigating as possible lies. Also, don't forget the broken water formed by obstructions like exposed boulders or trailing vegetation.

Tributaries

Tributary streams or springs often bring into the main river different water qualities that can attract salmon. Springs bring warmer water into a very cold river, and cooler water into a very warm one. Silt-carrying streams or run-offs might put some colour in otherwise gin-clear summer flows. Fast tributaries can recharge stretches of river with newly oxygenated water during warm low-water periods. So pay attention to the water below the junctions of tributaries for improved fishing conditions. Where I fish in summer, salmon often run up under the bubble stream that flows from the mouth of a fast little tributary. This is always prime taking water when it's hot.

The Bottom

I don't pay much attention to this, but some anglers do. Mixed rubble, rocks, gravel and boulders from fist-size and up are thought to be best. Sandy bottoms are thought to be less good, because fish don't like getting sand in their gills.[44]

What is the Water Temperature?

If you are going to keep track of anything when it comes to fishing conditions, water temperature ought to be it. If you don't have a thermometer, get one and use it often. It doesn't have to be anything hi-tech or electronic; a simple, cheap house thermometer with some tape wrapped around one end to protect the glass bulb and a string tied to the other works fine.

Knowing the water temperature tells much about where fish are likely to be on any stretch of river, and what kind of shape they will be in to respond to your lure. Remember, salmon like cool water around 45–55°F (7–13°C). Warmer or colder than that and they'll begin to adjust their behaviour, so to be effective you will need to adjust yours accordingly. Colder than ideal means more lethargic, slower, less agile, deeper-lying and deeper-running fish. So, fishing bigger, brighter, slower and deeper is usually the key to taking them. Warmer than ideal means faster, edgier, more sensitive, aggressive and easily spooked fish that often lie and run higher up in the water. Fishing smaller, duller, higher and faster can be the solution. Also, warm water holds less oxygen than cold water. Hence, in warm water you'll often find fish in faster flows, where they can get more water (and oxygen) through their gills faster; but when it's colder they can breathe well enough even in slow currents.

How High is the Water?

Salmon and sea trout anglers talk a lot about high water, low water and prime – or ideal – water. These are actually shorthand terms for how a river's flow height, strength and clarity vary. This is important because it affects how well salmon can see our lure (and so the size of the strike zone), whether they are feeling secure or aggressive enough to take it once they have, and also when and where they are most likely to lie and to run.

All rivers rise and fall and vary in water clarity, due to rainfall, snow melt, erosion, tides, or because they're regulated by dams. Some streams and rivers can go from low-and-clear to high-and-muddy in a matter of hours, others rise and fall over days or weeks.

After water temperature, water height (i.e. height, strength and clarity) should be your second tactical consideration. I start by taking a good look at the river and asking myself some questions. Does the flow seem normal? Is the river running in its bed or higher up on the banks? Is it flooding the shallows and inlets or trickling along deep in the middle of the bed?

Watching familiar water over time you'll get a feel for these changes. Is it falling? Rising? You can check the bank or rocks for wetness. You can also look more closely for the surface tension of the water where it comes into contact with a feature. If it is sagging, the water is falling; if it's bulging, then the water is rising. Most rivers have height gauges somewhere – often on bridge pilings. Take a reading if you can find one. Or make a mark on a boulder and check water level against it periodically.

The standard way to check for water clarity is by seeing how far you can see through it. Can you see the bottom? Can you see your boot tips when you're standing waist deep in it? Not that deep? The first thing I usually do is toss my lure in, then see how far down it sinks before I lose sight of it. Two feet (60 cm)? Three feet (1 m)? Six feet (1.8 m)? Remember, whatever the visual distance, you'll need to get your lure *closer than that* to have a chance of eliciting a strike out of a near-sighted salmon. I also use the opportunity to see whether my lure selection seems right for the water in terms of brightness and colour.

Water height, strength and clarity vary across a continuum, of course. But for angling purposes I've found it's usually sufficient to break it up into three kinds of water: high, prime, and low.

High Water

Water highly coloured to muddy, flowing high and fast; visual range (angler's) under 3 ft (1 m); strike zone under 18 in (45 cm). Expect fish to lie along edges and deeper pockets or to run along current breaks or seams in daylight, often close to shore.

Prime Water

Water coloured (pale lager beer/very weak coffee); visual range 3–6 ft (1–1.8 m); strike zone 1½–3 ft (0.5–1 m). Expect fish to be spread out across the river in normal lies, possibly running at any hour.

Low Water

Water clear; visual range over 6 ft (1.8 m); strike zone 3–6 ft (1–1.8 m). Edgy, skittish, easily spooked fish lying in broken water during the day and in deeper pools by night; if the flow is sufficient, running after dark.

How About the Water Surface?

A choppy or broken surface always fishes better than a calm flat one, because fish feel less exposed, more secure, and so take more easily. If you are fishing a clear, smooth pool or glide, try to stay concealed or, better yet, fish it from dusk to dawn or on a cloudy day.

How Light Is It?

Salmon, like trout, shun direct bright light (see Juell and Fossei-dengen). In clear water on a bright day they will run less and lie up where it's shady; look for them in deeper glides, pool necks, and under riffles. If the light is lower, say dusk to dawn, or on cloudy, overcast or rainy days, they will run more freely and higher up in the water; look for them in the heads and tails of pools and in the slower seams, sometimes close in to the shore.

How About the Weather?

Salmon aren't nearly as sensitive to weather changes as sea trout seem to be. So, except for its effects on water and light levels, I don't pay too much attention to it. Still, there are some conditions to watch for. One is when you are fishing in cold water – say, 30–45°F (-1–7°C) on a sunny day. By about midday the sun can warm things up enough to kick-start cold lethargic fish into action and bring on the bite. A warm breeze can do the same. The other situation is when you're fishing in warm, low, clear water at night. A chilly breeze can cool the water just enough to stimulate warm fish into activity so they take better. Hugh Falkus noted the chilly conditions that often attended catching salmon at night: 'a thick ground mist, with accompanying drop in temperature' (1984, p. 202). This is another instance where salmon differ from sea trout. Quick drops in air temperature often put sea trout into a temporary stupor – not salmon, it seems.

Time of Day?

In warm weather, salmon are almost always more active from dusk to dawn when it's coolest. So those are times to be on the water if you're looking for good chances to hook one. In colder weather look to dawn and dusk for periods of activity and better fishing, and – if it's sunny – also to midday.

Can I Actually See Fish?

Some people like to fish to salmon they can see. Obviously it cuts out a lot of search time when you know your target. I don't mean glimpsed surface shows, but fish you can actually see below the surface. For me, this is a mixed blessing. When I've got a fish in my sights I tend to spend too much time on it, when I'd probably do better moving on to new targets. Some anglers, though, get a kick out of working a fish over until they get a reaction[45] (I guess I'm too impatient). But no one can tell you how long to stay on a target: you need to make that call yourself.

Where Is the Action?

Every trout angler learns that there are definite advantages to being the first rod on a pool: calm, undisturbed trout simply take better. It's often the first angler through who ends up with the lion's share of trout. Not so with salmon. To be sure, spooked and frightened salmon aren't going to respond well to a lure. But slightly agitated, unsettled, even angry salmon might. It's well known among seasoned anglers that, as the saying goes, you calm a sea trout to bite, but you agitate a salmon.

This also means, all aesthetics aside, that with salmon following the crowd can be a good tactical move. Anglers walking along the bank, wading, plopping hardware into the water; boat fishers passing by, even hooking and playing fish – all can shake up the settled order of things along any piece of water and make salmon fishing *better*. Remember, an unsettled salmon, an agitated salmon, a salmon that's been forced to relocate is a more aggressive fish, and that's going to be a taking fish![46] I've seen it plenty of times: one angler hooks a fish, another nearby soon follows, then another – the bite is on! Some anglers fish to get away on their own. Fine. But if you're looking to take salmon and you're not averse to a little company, try going where the action is.

Are There Tides?

Most of your fishing is probably going to be far enough upriver that you don't have to think about tides. But if you're fishing near the mouth you'll need to. First, it's at the upper limits of high-tide water, where salt mingles with fresh, that salmon will lie for a time – days to weeks – while they readjust their body chemistry to deal with fresh water before moving upriver. Second, salmon tend to migrate from the estuary on the outgoing (or receding) tides. So knowing how, when and where the tidal currents move can be essential if you want to be in the right place at the right time. Start by getting yourself a good tide table and a set of detailed bathymetric (bottom contour) maps of the river mouth and estuary.

What About Stealth?

Everybody agrees that salmon aren't as easily spooked as trout. But you shouldn't push your luck. They will take a lure when agitated, not when they are frightened. A salmon has acute vision and smell. You need to be careful when the water is clear and calm, especially in dull conditions or half-light, when fish see best. Try not to stand out against the background, move along the shore low and slow, wade deep or stay back from the water's edge, and try to cover a lie with a long line from downstream. Talking, shouting, even thumping rocks while wading, or rumbling around inside your boat probably aren't going to put salmon off. But the sight of you will. A fish might not vanish when it sees you. But the chances are it won't take your lure. Remember also that certain odours *will* make salmon turn tail and flee. Make sure these aren't part of your offering (see 'How About Smell?', p. 54).

Which Lures and Presentations Should I Use?

Once you've taken care of the preliminaries you can settle into thinking about what and how to fish. Think first about lure size, action, colour, and pattern; think in terms of your lure's visibility, given the prevailing water clarity and light, and whether it's going to attract or spook fish, bearing in mind the water temperature/fish metabolism equation. Then think about presentation – speed, depth, path, etc., and about what kind of rigging you'll need so you can put your lure in the strike zone.

Can I Get Help?

Don't be shy: ask along the river. Talk to boat fishers who have just come in. In my experience spinning-anglers tend to be more sociable than fly-fishers and like to talk about their catches, gear and tactics. Listen and learn! You can also go the whole hog and hire a ghillie or guide. In any event, you should start any campaign at the local tackle shop. These are the clearing houses for local gossip, the contact points for expert help, and the purveyors of lures known to be effective locally.

Tip: Good taking conditions

If you're looking to schedule the most promising times to be on the river, the master himself, Hugh Falkus (1984, p.152) summarized what to look for and what to avoid:

> ...the first essential is a stock of fresh-run fish. Then the river must be at a good height, with the water temperature around 50°F (10°C). And since dull days are better than bright days, we want a dull, warm day with high cloud ceiling. Generally speaking, river conditions are good when:

1) The water temperature is rising steadily between 40–56°F (4.5–13°C), or dropping when above 57°F (14°C).
2) When the water height holds steady for a good length of time.
3) When the water is starting to rise (for the first 6 in (15 cm)) after a drought.
4) When the water is dropping after a spate.

Fishing is poor when:

1) Mist is coming off the water ('haar'). Usually in the early morning or evening.
2) The air temperature is much colder than the water temperature: say a difference of 15°F (9.5°C).
3) A very bright sun is shining straight downstream into the salmon's eyes.
4) A strong gusty wind is blowing in squalls, with rapidly changing light. Very few fish are caught in these conditions, no matter whether the wind is blowing up or down the river.
5) The river is in full spate, with weed, grass, logs etc. coming downstream. This is the worst of all and usually hopeless for fishing.

How I Would Fish It

As a way of summarizing what's been said about lures, presentations and tactical considerations, I'll put down some thoughts on how I'd fish the more common situations anglers run into on a river. Because water temperature is the single most valuable piece of information you can have, I'll break it down in terms of tactics for cool-, warm-, and cold-water situations.

Cool-water Tactics

Temperatures around 45–55°F (7–13°C) are ideal for the spin-angler.[47] Fish are speedy, agile, aggressive and about as takeable as they ever will be on hardware. My main concerns when fishing in these temperatures will be the height and clarity of the water and how much light there is. On many rivers, ideal temperatures come in spring and autumn. This is also when there are periods of very high, dirty water due to melting snow and rain.

Cool, High Water in Daylight

When the river is bursting its banks and the water is running so brown you can't see more than 2 ft (60 cm) through it, I know the chances of good fishing are going to be limited. But I'm usually too impatient to wait for better, so I'll try and make the most of it, even if it means fishing in the rain. At least there's one thing going for me: most of the salmon will be concentrated along the slower edges of the main current – in the current breaks or seams – sometimes only a few feet offshore.

How I work the seams in high water is going to depend on whether or not I see any signs of fish moving – showing on the surface, jumping or rolling. If not, I'll try backing my biggest lure – probably a heavy spoon – down this strip flatline. If the water isn't too strong and intimidating, and the seam's not too far out, I'll wade in so I can work the lure straight downstream below me. Since I know the strike zone is going to be less than 1 ft (30 cm) in this soup, I'll aim to put the lure literally in the fish's face. I'll try

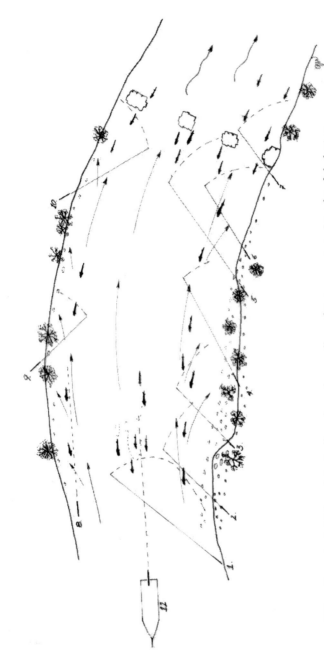

When the water is high and, typically, coloured, regardless of its temperature, I tend to fish during the day and concentrate on covering the near-shore seams with short sweeps or backing a lure down from a wading position (2,3,4,8,9), and any deeper pockets further out also with sweeps from shore (1) or by backing a lure down from my anchored boat (11). I'll also fish the water thoroughly around any structures like old bridge pilings that might provide cover (5,6,7,10).

to keep it bouncing along the bottom backwards in little steps, so, ideally, the fish either has to take it or move out of its way!

If I do see signs of fish moving up the seam, though, I'll think of intercepting them. I might stay with a flatline set-up and try hanging a lure in the current at about mid-depth. I'll try a spoon first – skinny or fat depending on the strength of the current. If I can't keep it fishing at the right depth, I'll change to a ledger rig so I can hang (plunk) a big garish thin-blade spoon or maybe a big Devon or diving plug. Whether backing down or plunking, I'll work the seam a section at a time – covering 20 yd (18 m) say, then repositioning.

If the seam is too far out to wade to safely, I might use my harling boat for better positioning. I'll motor up the middle of the river, pull over into the seam, drop anchor and fish it the same as I would on foot, backing down or plunking a strip of seam, then pulling anchor and dropping down again.

I know there will also be some fish lying in deeper water further out where structures like boulders, logs, pilings, etc., give protection from the current. With the boat I can also try for them. In high water I might not be able to see any traces of these lies, but with any luck I'll remember their position from lower-water days. I'll either anchor or hold the boat against the current with the outboard above these lies and fish them the same as I did the seams. If I'm having trouble keeping my lure down in the heavier water, I'll switch to a ledger rig.

Whatever lure I decide on, it will be decked out for maximum visibility, with high-contrast patterns like the orange-and-white tiger.

Cool, High Water, Dusk to Dawn

That's daylight methods, and I might work them right up till sunset. After that, though, I can't expect much action. It's just too hard for salmon to detect a lure in high, dirty water when the light's gone. Sensible spinners head off home or to the pub. The rest of us soldier on into the darkness for another hour on the outside chance of a take.

Under these conditions there's really only one chance of success: working a big, loud and preferably smelly lure down a seam in the hope of making contact with a running fish. I could use the same lures I did in daylight. But I have a lure I've made for just these times. It's a big thin-blade spoon – silver or gold on the inside, orange-and-white tiger pattern outside, about 4–5 in (10–12 cm) long. (Glow-paint works even better, but I don't seem to have the patience any more to keep it recharged.[48]) If I remembered to pack some PowerBait dough I'll lather on as much as the spoon will carry and still wobble; if I haven't, I'll see if I can scavenge a shrimp tail left by a bait angler and stick that on the treble.

I'll look for a stretch where the water runs very near the bank and not more than a few feet deep where I reckon my lure's got a better chance of meeting a fish. Sometimes I can pull this off flat-line, but I usually change to a dropper-weight set-up. As in daylight, I'll try to wade out (or anchor my boat) so I can work the spoon very slowly down the seam below me, hanging it at intervals for as long as my patience lasts. This is certainly shooting in the dark, but sometimes I do manage to hit a fish!

Cool, Prime Water in Daylight

Once the water has dropped down to near normal height and cleared so you can see about 3–6 ft (1–2 m) through it, conditions are pretty much ideal. No excuses now! There is still enough colour in the water, so fish feel secure and can be active around the clock, but the current isn't as strong, so fish will spread out across more lies and use more of the water column. Hence the key to success is going to be good coverage.

The current seam is still the best bet, so I'll cover that first. It'll be a wider strip now, and maybe too far out to wade to. Still, I'll try to get close enough to cover it with a series of sweeps. I'll try flatline first. If I don't see signs of running fish I'll keep my offering deep and slow, even bumping the bottom. But if fish are moving I'll try to cover more of the column by jig-sweeping. Depending on the depth in the seam, I might make one pass deep, then one higher up.

A spoon a little smaller than the one I used in high water will be my first choice. If it's sunny or fairly clear I'll go with something silver, pearl, chrome nickel, gold or polished brass or copper – with a little bit of red or orange for added visibility. Probably it will be

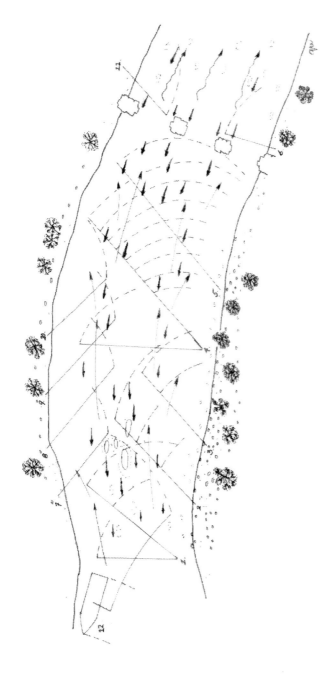

Prime water deserves thorough coverage in all temperatures. I'll usually start by covering the now wider seams, and any deeper pockets or potential lies around structures that provide cover – working down with short sweeps from shore (1,2,3,4,6,7,8,9,10,11) or from my harling boat (12). I'll leave the pool tail until dusk and cover it thoroughly, sweeping to a grid (4,5).

either my pearl and red-orange Mobacken, or my silver, black and orange Fattail (see Appendix for how to make them).

These are prime conditions for harling too, so I may pull the boat out. If I feel like exercise, I'll row upriver above a nice stretch of target water. Then I'll drift (back-troll) down a seam in intervals, anchoring for a time above likely lies. For the drift, my first choice is usually a heavy spoon jigged flatline in steps along the bottom. If there's a nice pool, I'll anchor at the head so I can work over the neck water. I may cover it jig-sweeping with the same tackle, but I've had better luck switching to a dropper-weight rig so I can drift-ledger a thin-blade spoon, diving plug or minnow – whichever strikes my fancy at the time.

If I don't feel like rowing, I'll screw on the outboard. The motor makes for easier fishing, and it also let's me cover a lot more water in the same time. For the deep glides and long pool necks it's hard to beat up-current trolling. Where the seams are wide or hard to see at all I've had good results simply following the bottom contours really slowly. Where the current break is clear, I'll fish up the middle of the seam instead. The local standard for this work is either a Ripplin' Red Fin in orange with a gold belly, or a Rapala original – one piece or jointed – in gold with a red back. Sometimes I fish a home-made J-plug instead.

Coming back down I usually back-troll the same ledgered diving plug. Or, for a change, maybe I'll tie on a thin-blade spoon. Using the motor to check my drift speed I can scour the river nearly bank to bank and feel pretty sure I've covered most of the fish around.

Cool, Prime Water, Dusk to Dawn

The water is still too coloured to fish well in darkness, but salmon usually go on the take in the fading light of dusk, so I'll make sure I've got a lure in the water for that. I'll still target seams further out, but, now the light is low, I can expect fish to be running in shallower currents near the shore too. I'll be careful to cover these first, before wading out.

I'll work down-current as before, covering the strip in short sweeps. I'll still use spoons, but I might bump them up a size and go for a higher-contrast pattern – black-and-white, blue-and-white, black-and-orange – for added visibility. If there are lots of fish showing I'll stay high, or I'll jig-sweep like before. I've found I often get a take when I'm bringing the lure back home up the strip, stop-and-go style.

Pool tails are prime targets too. Running fish will rest in the shallow, flat water just above the sill or break. So I'll spend time covering these thoroughly. I'll try positioning above – wading out if I can – so I can cover every square yard/metre of water with big, curving sweeps using the same lures.

If I'm in my boat I'll cover these same lies from an anchored position. Using the motor I can also troll up- and down-current between them, as I did in daylight. If I see fish showing, especially on the flatter glides, I'll probably fish two rods up-current, one ledger-rigged and fishing deep, one flatline and fishing a spoon, diving plug, or Devon higher up. I might back-troll a single rod coming home.

Cool, Low Water in Daylight

Even during spring and autumn there can be days when the water runs low and clear. If I wanted to be efficient about this I'd stay off the water when it's bright and fish it dusk to dawn when the odds are better. But the chances are I won't be able to wait, so it's a question of making the most of the daylight. If it's a little overcast, my chances are better. I'd be surprised if fish were running when the water is this low and clear, so I'll mainly target secure lies, the deeper glides, the pool necks. I'll work these down deep-sweeping, or jig-sweeping – probably using the same medium-size spoon I fished in prime water – maybe on foot, or maybe from my anchored boat. These fish are going to be a little warier than they were when the water had some colour in it, but still not as edgy as they are when it's warmer. Still, I'll be thinking stealthy – staying low, casting long and trying not to cause too much disturbance.

Cool, Low Water, Dusk to Dawn

If the day's been bright and sunny, and the fishing pretty slow, I'll look forward to it picking up once the sun's off the water. With

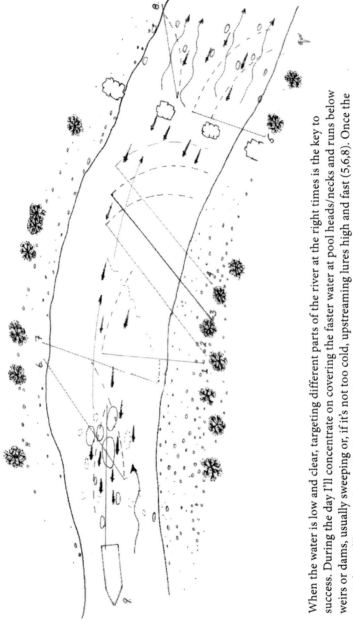

When the water is low and clear, targeting different parts of the river at the right times is the key to success. During the day I'll concentrate on covering the faster water at pool heads/necks and runs below weirs or dams, usually sweeping or, if it's not too cold, upstreaming lures high and fast (5,6,8). Once the sun is down I'll sweep the pool tail thoroughly (2,3,4). If fish are showing in the glides I'll try ripping from shore (7) or harling (9). I'll leave the deeper water of glides and pool bellies until dawn (1).

ideal water temperatures like this the last hour of daylight can mean good fishing! I figure the fish that have been holed up all day are going to start moving, and they'll be my first targets. The pool tails are the place to start. By half an hour before sunset I'll be in position, so I can sweep the tail thoroughly with a silver spoon, something with some black-and-white, black-and-orange, or black-and-blue on it for added contrast. I'll wade into position, or else I'll cast from my boat anchored to one side near the head of the pool. I'll start my sweeps just below the pool's belly and work down to the break. If there are fish showing in the glides I'll cover these too. The flow will probably be too weak to back-troll effectively, but drift-jigging a Fathead might be worth a try.

Many anglers pack up and head home once it's got dark. And on some rivers that's the law.[49] If I'm tired and/or I've got a fish already, I'll do the same. If not, I might fish on for an hour or so until it gets too cold to be much fun. In my experience, cool-water fish continue to run after dark – at least for the first couple of hours. They will also run tight along the shore in water only a couple of feet deep, if there's enough current. I've caught them there bringing a spoon back home stop-and-go.

Warm-water Tactics

When water gets to around 55°F (13°C) and higher I'm thinking in terms of quick, edgy, aggressive, high-metabolism fish looking for cooler, better-oxygenated water. Fly-fishers do well in these temperatures. To keep up with them, I'll need to adjust my hardware tactics. Still, as long as the water stays below 70°F (21°C), salmon will strike savagely, fight hard, leap acrobatically and even chase down a lure over a good distance – sometimes right to your feet! Warmer than that though, and fish go into survival mode: little movement and little interest in much else but breathing.

Warm, Low Water in Daylight

If the water gets as warm as this, it's usually fairly low too. If I'm out in full daylight, and the water is very clear, the spook factor comes into play in a big way. So, whatever I do, I know I've got to stay low, keep quiet and try to blend in. I'll probably fish mainly the faster, bouncier stretches at head-ins and riffles below pools, and the frothy water under falls and spills. The bubble streams below tributaries are also worth a shot. These targets may only be 2–3 ft (60–90 cm) deep, but it's where I'll look for fish seeking mid-day refuge in broken, better-oxygenated and slightly cooler water.

This is when upstreaming a lure high and fast with the current comes into its own. But these are edgy fish, and really easy to over-stimulate, so smaller, duller lures are the order of the day. A copper Toby in the ⅕–⅓ oz (4–10 g) range with a black zebra pattern, and home-made silver spoon-handle spoons in black and orange are two of my favourites for this work.

Keeping a spoon or spinner fishing at the right speed in really shallow bouncy runs can be a challenge. That's why float-fishing was invented! So if I'm having trouble upstreaming these runs flat-line, I'll try drifting a small fat spoon, maybe even a small blade spinner off a float rig like they do on Pacific Coast rivers (see 'Fishing On Foot With Floats: Float or Bobber Fishing', p. 93).

If I feel like boating, I may motor down to the river mouth looking for deeper, cooler channels between 10 and 25 ft (3 and 7.5 m) deep. I'll be targeting salmon waiting for higher water before running upriver. Back-trolling a spinner, thin-blade spoon or plug deep on the ebbing tide sometimes works, even when it's blazing hot on the surface.

Warm, Low Water, Dusk to Dawn

Daylight fishing in warm low water is always better when it's cloudy, even drizzling, because it means slightly cooler water, lower light and more secure, active, aggressive and takeable fish. Other-wise, my best sport will come once the sun goes down. The last hour of sunlight through dusk is the traditional evening taking time, and I'll try to make that. Unless there has been a drought, so the water is barely running, the fish should begin to move once the sun is off the water, so I'll watch for their tail slaps, surface rolls and leaps. I'll forget about the fast water I've been working all day and target the calmer flows of glides and the heads and tails of pools instead.

Running fish will stop to rest in flat tail-water before entering the main pool, then again near the head before surging up through another run. High-sweeping a small light spoon, or maybe a spinner, is my standard move for these lies. If I see salmon nipping at things on the surface I'll be tempted to rig up with an in-line weight or buoyant casting bomb and to tie on the smallest lure I can find. A tiny gold, brass or copper spoon, a spinner with simple black-and-orange patterns, maybe a black-and-gold Devon – all under 1 in (2.5 cm) in length – have worked for me at times.

In the deeper glides, I'll look for running fish showing along the current seams and work over these too with short sweeps or jigging-sweeps a few feet at a time. Since this is faster water, and the light is getting pretty low, I'll change to something a little bigger – normally a medium-size spoon or spinner with some con-trasting pattern – the tiger for example, in fluorescent red-and-white, fluorescent orange-and-black, or blue-and-white.

Ripping is another option, if I'm not too tired. A 1 oz (28 g) Abu Koster painted black with a few fluorescent orange dots has long been my favourite for this. If there's enough room along the bank to manoeuvre without annoying too many of my fellow anglers I'll try to keep moving: throw-and-go I call it. I'll cast, rip off a strip of water – from bank to bank if I can reach it – then walk down a few paces and cast again. But if I'm hemmed in on both sides and there are enough fish showing on the surface, I'll switch to target mode. I'll wait for a rise, make my cast a few yards upstream of the spot and let rip. I want the spoon to flutter down just in front of and above that fish. Both modes have worked for me at times.

The foregoing assumes I'm on foot. But when it's warm and balmy there's nothing I like better than taking my boat out for the evening shift. The outboard stays in the garage, so I slip out into the river under oars like an old-time harler. I use the same tackle set-up as I would for flatlining the same lures – small spinners and spoons, maybe a J-plug or Devon with an in-line weight.

Once out in midstream I cast as long a line as I can over the stern, lean the rod behind the rowlock and start rowing slowly up-current. I manoeuvre in big wide S's, so my lure snakes across the water within 1 ft (30 cm) of the surface. If it's a smooth glide I'll work from bank to bank covering as much water as possible. In faster stretches I'll try to follow the current breaks in shorter S's, so the lure fishes back and forth across the seam. Following the foam line helps me keep on track when the light starts to go.

Once I've bitten off as much river as I want – or tired of rowing – I might drop anchor and try working over the seam by casting for a while. I usually fish back downriver the same way I did coming up, though if it's not yet too dark I might try jigging a heavy spoon while the boat drifts freely. I don't catch too many salmon this way, but it's always thrilling to play a big fish alone in a dinghy at dusk. At the very least I get some exercise!

I can't say much from experience about night-time fishing. On northern rivers in summer it never gets completely dark, so we fish in twilight right on through till dawn. But from what I've read, salmon can be taken in the dark. Hugh Falkus and his friends, who probably spent more summer nights on the river than in bed, reported taking salmon while fishing for sea trout in the small hours of morning. Falkus makes the point that all these salmon were caught under similar circumstances: all lying either at the heads of pools in 3–6 ft (1–1.8 m) of water, or in shallower water at the tail; all had sloshed on the surface just before taking (so we're dealing here with active fish); and all hit Falkus's own big Sunk Lure – a silver, blue and black fly of about 3 in (7.5 cm), which was sweeping high and fairly fast anywhere from 6–12 in (15–30 cm) under the surface. No surprises here. As long as salmon stay active at night, there's no reason they won't nail a lure sweeping right overhead even in pitch darkness, so long as they can see it.

Hitting deeper water at the crack of dawn can also be a good ploy, especially if temperatures have dipped overnight. If so, cooler, newly oxygenated water will sink into the deeper, calmer holes, and fish will follow. This is one of the few times that working over the deep belly of a pool can pay off. My normal tactic is to sneak up to the lower edge of the pool, staying as low as I can if the water is dead clear. I'll try covering these fish first by upstreaming a small spoon or spinner fairly fast a few feet above their heads. If that produces nothing, I'll move up further and try jig-sweeping a heavier spoon – probably a silver Fathead – right in front of their noses. These will be passive fish, so they won't be easy to rouse. Still, the occasional game fish makes it worth getting up that early. Once the sun's on the water, though, these holes will empty of fish. So I'll shift into daylight mode, working the faster water.

Warm, High Water in Daylight

Even during a hot dry summer, a heavy rain in the headwaters can put the river in spate, so it runs high and dirty. Hopefully the surge will bring some cooler water with it. If I'm going to fish it at all, I do just as I would under cooler conditions. I work the near-shore seams down-sweeping, ledgering, backing down, plunking (either wading or from my anchored boat) a big, garish spoon, a Devon or a diving plug. I'll hit the deeper pockets further out too, and work around any structures where a fish might be taking refuge from the current.

Warm, High Water, Dusk to Dawn

Same thing. These are pretty hopeless conditions, but if I'm feeling up to the challenge I'll fish as I would when it's a bit cooler: plunking my biggest, loudest and smelliest thin-blade in a near-shore seam at about mid-depth. When it gets dark, I'll quit.

Warm, Prime Water in Daylight

Once the water drops back down and clears a little, the odds of a take increase. I'll fish the water just as I do when it's cooler (see above), only now, I'll compensate for the warmer conditions by reducing the lure size a notch, and fishing a little faster and a little higher.

Warm, Prime Water, Dusk to Dawn

Even though it's warm, the chance of action goes right up once the light goes down. I'll fish the water much as I do when it's cooler, right on through dusk until it's good and dark. Prime targets will be running fish. I'll work the current breaks and pockets further out, the seams closer in, and the pool tails – on foot or from my anchored boat. Again, a high-sweeping spoon will be the main weapon – maybe a little bigger than I would use in full daylight and with a little more contrast, maybe black-and-white, blue-and-white or black-and-orange. If I'm boating, I might work the glides up and down too, top-trolling spoons, diving plugs or Devons.

Cold-water Tactics

By the time the water has dropped to 30–45°F (-1–7°C), I've usually already turned all my attention to the schools of fat shiny sea trout that have come into fresh water to overwinter. But if there's a late run of young grilse salmon I might retool and try for a nice one for the Christmas table. Or I might stick to sea trout right through the winter and wait for the ice to leave the banks before trying for a bright, fresh-run springer.

Whether I'm after winter grilse or springers, I'll follow the cardinal rules for cold-water salmon: low and slow, big and loud. Once the water gets down to around 35°F (1.5°C) I know I'm looking at a fish with about half the speed and twice the reaction time of its normal self. I may see a running fish showing now and then, but I'll ignore it. Most salmon will be deep, so that's where I'll be placing my bets – and lures. Since I don't like changing lures when it's this cold, I'll stick to a few tried-and-true spoons to get me through the season, probably a Mobacken, a Fattail, or a thin-blade. Since my boat will be 'dry-docked' for winter, I'll be fishing on foot.

Cold, Low Water in Daylight

These are typical early-winter conditions, but cold fish are less edgy fish, so I know my chances of hooking one are good even during bright daylight. This late in the season there are also plenty of fish around. And with spawning time getting close, they'll be getting more and more aggressive. I believe any lure that invades a territory now runs a good risk of getting attacked. But I also know fresh-run grilse will be outnumbered by older fish. Most of these will be highly coloured mature spawners in poor to very poor condition, so I'll count on returning maybe five fish for every one I keep.

I'll focus on covering the deeper pools and glides where these cold and less than athletic fish can rest more easily and securely when not running. A big (1 oz/28 g) pearl Mobacken with a blue or red-orange stripe is my first choice. If I can't keep that fishing deep enough, I'll tie on a heavier (1¼–1½ oz/35–45 g) silver Fattail with a white-and-black pattern. I'll try to scour the bottom by deep-sweeping to a grid, so I can cover as many fish as possible. About half my cold-water fish have hit the lure at the bend, the other half when I'm inching it back home from the dangle.

Cold, Low Water, Dusk to Dawn

Unless I'm too cold, I'll keep this routine up right through dusk. Even in freezing temperatures you can usually count on fish getting a little more active for about thirty minutes before the sun hits the horizon. If I don't yet have a fish on the bank, I'm pretty sure I can land one before it gets dark. Either way, by then, me and my tackle will be getting too cold to operate reliably, and that will be that for the day.

Cold, Prime Water in Daylight

With a little more colour in the water, daylight fishing usually gets better. I'll work the water the same as I do when it's clearer, but I might choose a slightly hotter-colour pattern to help with visibility: fluorescent orange with black for contrast looks good.

If I can only get out for an hour or two, I'll try to be on the water from about 11 till 1 o'clock. Some of my cronies will be munching sandwiches and sipping hot coffee about then, but I'll be fishing. By midday the sun often warms things up just enough to encourage some fish to run. And I'll see if I can cover one. My favourite ploy for lunchtime runners is deep jig-sweeping in glides and seams with one of my Fantails, then inching it back home from the dangle. Lunch always tastes better when I've got a fish on the bank.

Cold, Prime Water, Dusk to Dawn

Even a little colour in the water seems to be too much when it's cold and the light gets low. Cloudy days are usually pretty slow, and any taking spell that does come on at dusk seems to last no more than about fifteen minutes. Still, the fish will be moving, so I'll be working the seams to try and connect with one. I'll try sweeping them – same spoons, fishing flatline – or I might rig up a ledger weight and try hanging or backing down a big garish thin-blade spoon.

Cold, High Water in Daylight

This is typical water during the spring melt: high, dirty and really cold, sometimes with the added twist of floating ice. Nasty conditions for being out, really. But this is when the first springers arrive – fat, healthy and pure silver – and, if you can put your lure on the nose of one, you might be into your best fish of the year. Something big, slow and garish is going to be the key. I could fish flatline, but ledgering will be more efficient so I rig up for that. Fish are moving up; I'm setting ambushes. Wading might be an option, or I'll look for bends and points along the water where I can work down a seam from straight above it – hanging, backing down, even plunking. The local fly-fishers will all be fishing big orange and black General Practitioners (GPs). I'll be going with a spinner's version, a big gold thin-blade with a fluorescent orange tiger pattern.

Cold, High Water, Dusk to Dawn

Connecting with a salmon when the light's fading and in water that allows near zero visibility is always a long shot. Add the fish's slow metabolism/reaction time, and the chances are even more remote. Yes, I could go to work with my big orange tiger thin-blade – but my cold feet and hands tell me it's not worth it. Maybe tomorrow!

Appendix: Making Your
Own Spinning Baits

I can think of lots of reasons for making your own spinning baits. Here are four good ones. First, it's educational. Making lures gives you a better understanding of how they work and why – and that's got to make you a better angler. Most fly-anglers make their own lures; more spin-anglers should too. A second reason is cost reduction. Everybody loses lures from time to time; you simply can't fish a lure effectively without running that risk. If you fish waters like I do, where the bottom gobbles up lures like peanuts, then fishing shop-bought baits can make a real dent in your wallet. So making your own lures at a fraction of the cost makes good sense. A third reason is performance. Making a lure means controlling its design, how it looks and how it works. It lets you customize a lure to your specific needs. I'm not talking about making lures that are nearly as good as shop-bought specimens, but about making them better! Finally, catching fish on a lure you've made yourself – maybe even designed yourself – brings its own kind of satisfaction, not to mention building your confidence as an angler.

But I'll be realistic. It's much easier to make some types of lures than others, and some types simply aren't worth the effort. It's much easier to make good spoons and minnows than good diving plugs, for example.

Spoons

Spoons are some of the simplest and most effective lures you can fish for river salmon. They are also about the easiest to make yourself. You have two options: assembling components you buy wholesale, and making spoon bodies from scratch.

Assembled Spoons

Many anglers buy spoon components and assemble them at home. Mail-order houses offer all the parts you need in bulk. All you do is attach the split rings and hook to the blank, and you have a complete spoon. You can usually order the spoon bodies with unfinished or polished surfaces. Nickel is the most common metal, brass and copper second; some companies carry genuine silver plate, a few even gold plate. Once they are assembled you can fish your spoons as is, or finish them off with paint or colour-pattern tape.

The only risk to buying wholesale components in bulk is maybe getting stuck with a dozen or more spoons that don't perform the way you hoped they would in the water. You can usually remedy this by altering the shape in a vice with pliers – called *tuning*. For example, if you want to dampen its action you can flatten the curvature, or tweak the hook arrangement (by adding an extra split ring, adding a bead, lead wire or twine to the shank, or go to a larger or smaller hook size). Even with the minor tuning and tweaking, buying components in bulk is usually still worth it.

The best way to find companies that sell spoon components is to search the Internet. Many of them also sell components for assembling spinners. Start by taking a look at the following distributors, also for hooks, rings, and colour-pattern tape:

Real Pro's SportFishing, PO Box 17, Hepworth, Ontario, Canada N0H 1P0. (www.luremaking.com)

Stamina Quality Components, 8401 73rd Ave. N, Unit 40, Brooklyn Park, Minneapolis MN 55428, USA. (www.staminainc.com)

YGA (Yorkshire Game Angling), online store only. (www.yga.yorks.com)

Making Found-metal Spoons From Scratch

Another option is making spoons from preshaped pieces of metal you find yourself. The best source for found-metal spoons I know is tableware. It's no coincidence we call these lures spoons! Remember the stories about discovery in Chapter 2? Not only spoon bowls, but the handles of spoons, knives and forks often have curvatures that can be cut out and used, either as is or after a little bending, to produce excellent salmon spoon bodies. You can find them in plain nickel, chrome nickel, stainless steel, real silver plate, even real gold plate.

As for sources, charity shops that carry used housewares are the first places to look. Local flea markets and auctions are also good, especially for silverware in bulk. These are all good places to find usable tableware for next to nothing, including real silver or gold plate if you're lucky.

Don't worry if the silver looks tarnished and ugly when you find it: a little work with a polishing cloth and it'll shine like new! Real silver or gold plate tableware makes great spoons for cold-water, high-light conditions. The lustre is unbeatable, and the greater density makes for good control and a more reliable action.

MATERIALS:

Hacksaw
Normal pliers
Metal file
Wire snips
Power drill with *c.* 3 mm bit made for drilling hard steel
Steel vice
Wire (*c.* 1 mm thick copper, steel or aluminium – I salvage mine from electrical cable), or split rings (from the tackle shop)
Found-metal source (i.e. spoons, knives, forks)
Treble hooks (sizes 4 and 6)
Silver polishing cloth

I've made hundreds of spoons from tableware. Some have worked better than others. Here are a few of them:

Spoon- and Fork-handle Spoons

Take a look at the handles on common spoons or forks and you'll
see they conform to three basic shapes: flat or slab, concave, or pin.
With a little reshaping they make good elongated spoon bodies.

CONSTRUCTION:

1. Cut the handle to the desired length with a hacksaw. You'll
   need to experiment a little to find the right length, width and
   density proportions to achieve the desired action in the kinds of
   water you fish. It will also depend on whether the piece is
   essentially a flat slab or concave, and what kind of bends you
   put into it (Step 3).

   For narrow, concave-handle spoons (nickel-based) three sizes
   have worked for me:

   > Length 1¾–2 in (45–50 mm), max. width ½ in (12 mm),
   >   approx. weight ³/₁₆ oz (5 g) (size 6 treble hook)
   > Length 2½ in (60 mm), max. width ½ in (12–14 mm),
   >   approx. weight ⅜ oz (10 g) (size 4 treble hook)
   > Length 3–3⅛ in (75–80 mm), max. width ½ in (12–14 mm),
   >   approx. weight ½ oz (15 g) (size 4 treble hook)
   > For wider, slab-handle spoons (silver plate) I make two
   > sizes:
   > Length 2⅛ in (55 mm), max. width ⅝ in (17 mm), approx.
   >   weight ⅝ oz (18 g) (size 4 treble hook)
   > Length 2¾ in (70 mm), max. width ¾ in (20 mm), approx.
   >   weight ⅞ oz (25 g) (size 4 treble hook)

2. Drill holes at both ends (*c.* 3 mm).
3. Put an S bend in the piece using a vice and pliers. You're going
   to make the bend in two parts. First, place the spoon blank in a
   steel vice with the front (narrower) end up. If it has a concave
   side, face that toward you. You want the vice to grip the piece
   about two thirds of the way down its length. Now grab the
   blank near the end with a pair of pliers and slowly bend it away
   from you. Not too much, only a little. Any concave surface
   should be on the outside of the bend. Next, take the piece out,
   turn it over and place it back in the vice, this time with about

one third of the length sticking out and any concave surface facing away from you. Grab the end with pliers and slowly bend the piece, again, away from you. Any concave surface should now be on the inside of the curve. The result should be a spoon body with gentle S-curvature. Take a look at any commercial Toby-like spoon to a get an idea of the curvatures you're aiming at.

4. Attach a treble hook to the wider end with a loop of wire or split ring; add a second to the narrower end for tying up to. Try a double loop at the treble attachment if fish seem to be throwing the hook.
5. Done. It's ready to fish! If it doesn't look the way it should in the water, you can tune it in the workshop. In time you'll get a feel for the curvatures you need to make it move the way you want it to.

The narrower concave nickel-based metal spoons are excellent for shallow presentations. I've used them with good results for high-sweeping and hanging in currents, as well as for harling and light trolling. I usually fish the lightest – $3/_{16}$ oz (5 g) – model off a ledger rig.

The wider, slab-bodied silver-plate spoons are some of the most versatile spoons I've ever fished. They seem to work equally well when drifted, swept, jigged or hung in currents. They also troll well at slower speeds.

I tend to fish both types in their natural finish, or with a little black tape for contrast.

Knife-handle Spoons

Spoons made from the handles of common table knives are among the most effective I've ever fished for salmon as well as trout, and almost too easy to make. You simply cut the handle from a table knife with a hacksaw, drill holes at both ends, attach a hook to one end and a split ring to the other, and you're ready to fish.

One reason knife handles work so well as spoon bodies is their density. A 4 in (100 mm)-long silver-plate handle weighs around

1½ oz (45 g), one 3½ in (85 mm) long around 1¼ oz (35 g); steel is a little lighter. So these lures sink quickly and stay down where you want them to be. A second reason is their shape. You can make serviceable spoons out of almost any knife. But the best have certain features. Look for handles that are fat and narrow at the blade end (squarish in cross-section) and wide and thin (lenticular in cross-section) at the butt end. Which end you attach the hook to and what kind of bend you hammer into it will largely determine what kind of action it has.

When I'm making a knife-handle spoon for jigging I want it to have a slight wiggle when it sinks and no real action when it's drawn. To get this I don't bend it at all, but I do attach the hook to the fatter, narrower end. I call it Fathead.

To turn this into a skinny spoon with a more regular, rhythmic action on the retrieve I make it differently. First I hammer a slight S-bend along the entire axis. Then I attach the hook to the wider, flatter end. I call this Fattail. It's served me as an exceptionally good spoon for both sea trout and salmon, especially for deep-sweeping presentations in heavy currents. I rig them both with a size 2 or size 4 treble, nowadays with a flying mount (see Chapter 2, 'Flying mount for skinny spoons', p. 40).

I've found I can increase their effectiveness by simply adding a metal flipper (I cut them out of tin-can metal) to the tail ring. Otherwise I fish them as is, in plain silver or nickel, or with a little black or blue marker or tape added for contrast.

Hand-moulded Spoons

Few anglers have the skills or heavy equipment to mould hard-metal spoon bodies themselves. But there are other options. One is working with softer, malleable metals like lead, tin or tungsten. Another is working with very thin sheet metals.

Soft-metal Spoons

Besides allowing you to build spoons of almost any shape, soft metals let you make spoon bodies that have some clear advantages. One is higher density. Lead, tin and tungsten spoons sink faster, cast further and have more stable actions than spoons of the same size in other metals. Another is tunability. Soft-metal spoons can be quickly reshaped by hand at the waterside to get them running just right. Finally, they are cheap and easy to make.

MATERIALS:

Sheet lead, tin or tungsten of about 2 mm thickness. Lead is the easiest to find and the cheapest to buy. Try salvage yards and recycling plants. But check for any lead-free regulations where you fish. Tungsten and tin are less toxic, and have about the same specific gravity (density) and similar malleability as lead. But they are harder to find and lot pricier. Search the Web for outlets.
Scriber. A nail or ice-pick works fine too
Sharp, thin-bladed chisel
Wire snips
Pliers
Hammer
Wire of *c*. 1 mm thickness in copper, steel or aluminium
Power drill with c. 3 mm steel-drilling bit
Sandpaper

CONSTRUCTION:

For making the spoon body there are two methods to choose from, depending on whether you want to make copies of existing spoons or create originals.

Making soft-metal copies of your favourite spoon bodies is the easiest. Here's how:

1. Take an identical pair of the spoon bodies you want to copy. These are your moulds (steel-bodied spoons make longer-lasting moulds than those of copper or brass).
2. Lay one spoon body on the lead or tungsten sheet, trace it and mark the position of the holes with a scriber.
3. Cut out the blank using a chisel and wire snips. Smooth the edges with sandpaper.

4. Drill holes (*c.* 3 mm) at both ends as marked.
5. Sandwich the cut blank between the spoon (mould) bodies. Nails slid through the lined-up holes will keep it all in place.
6. Squeeze the three layers of the sandwich together with pliers. Make sure you squeeze it all along its length until the soft-metal blank takes on the contours of the mould.
7. Prime the blank inside and out and let it dry. Ordinary water-based wall-paint primer works fine. Apply whatever paint you want to the primed surface.
8. Attach treble with a wire loop. You don't need a wire loop at the front end, since you can tie your leader directly into the front hole without fear of the soft metal cutting it.

Now for creating originals. I've experimented a great deal with different spoon body shapes. Here's a spoon that seems to work well for salmon. It's a wide-body oval or 'football' spoon I call the Mobacken. I've had great success with this fishing the deep glides along the Mobacken stretch of the Skellefteå river.

Mobacken spoon: Body length 2½ in (65 mm), body width (mid-point) 1 in (24 mm), approx. weight 1 oz (28 g).

CONSTRUCTION:

1. Instead of using an existing spoon body as a template, I start with a cardboard template cut to the intended football shape. Lay the template on the metal sheet, trace it with a scriber and cut out the blank. Remember to cut just *within* the scribed line, or the spoon will be too fat.
2. Drill holes (*c.* 3 mm) at both ends of the blank for attaching treble and line.
3. Clamp the blank in a steel vice. Position it lengthwise and as close along the central axis as you can; you should see half of each hole protruding above the vice. This is important to ensure the spoon's lateral symmetry and, ultimately, that it has the action you want in the water.
4. With a hammer, bend the half protruding above the vice a little. You don't need to be too precise here. You are looking for some-

thing in the region of 30–40° off the vertical. But do make sure you have bent it all along the axis from hole to hole. The result should be a piece of metal with a crease running down the axis. This crease forms the concave side (the side that rides up) of your spoon body.

5. Bend the blank lengthwise. You're going to do this by hand. You want to make a nice graceful S-curve with the bigger half of the curve toward the front and the smaller to the rear. Again, precision isn't important, because you can adjust the curvature easily at the waterside if it doesn't run the way you want it to.

6. Add a simple pattern. I paint the convex side only and leave the concave side natural metal (a dull silvery grey). Prime the outside (convex side) and let dry. Apply a coat of pearl white or silver paint, let dry. Add a stripe of red down one margin, let dry. You can also apply a layer of clear enamel to protect the paint.

7. Attach a size 2 or size 4 treble, either by a wire loop or a split ring.

8. Tie the line directly to the front hole via a loop knot (you don't need a front-end ring, because the soft-metal eye won't cut the line).

I should mention one obvious drawback to using soft metal for spoons: they are easily bent out of shape when pulling them loose from snags, and even when playing a heavy fish. Usually they can be restored to serviceable shape by hand at the waterside. Sometimes not. So it's always a good idea to carry several back-ups. I take badly bent spoons back to my workshop, cut off the hooks and reshape them for another day.

Tin-can-metal Spoons

I make a lot of my thin-blade spoons from tin-can metal. The main reason – besides saving money – is variety. Using normal casting spoons as templates and moulds I can make thin-blade spoons in a much wider range of shapes and sizes than I can easily find commercially. Also, since I fish them mainly in currents, I need to be able to test different types to find just the right fit for that particular piece of water. Besides, making them is easy.

MATERIALS:

Matched pair of steel spoon-bodies. These are your moulds.

Tin-can tops. You can use any thin metal that is easily cut. I use the metal tops from everyday tin cans, because the supply is free and almost unlimited, and also because the metal is both easy to work and resilient. In my experience, some can metals work better than others (they are all actually nickel-based alloys, not tin). But I find those with duller finishes to be more resilient than those with very shiny silver or gold-coloured finishes.

Sheet-metal cutters/tin snips. (Sheet-metal shears work fine; so do simple wire snips.)

Scriber (nail, ice-pick, etc.)

Pliers

Hammer

Wire (c. 1 mm thick copper, steel or aluminium), or split rings.

Treble hooks (sizes to fit spoon body)

Power drill with c. 3 mm bit

CONSTRUCTION:

This is nearly identical to making soft-metal spoon copies:

1. Choose the steel casting spoons you want to copy. You'll use one or two identical bodies, depending on whether you want a flat or convex-concave profile (see steps 6 and 7).
2. Cut the top (or bottom) from a tin can of large enough diameter.
3. With a hammer, flatten the can-top completely.
4. Lay one steel spoon body on the flattened can-top; outline it and mark the position of the holes with a scriber.
5. Cut out the spoon blank and sand the edges. (Be careful here; it's easy to cut yourself!)
6. To make a spoon with the same concave-convex profile as the original, use two identical spoon bodies as moulds. Sandwich the blank between the two spoon halves. Hold them in place by sticking nails through the holes.
7. Squeeze the three layers of the sandwich together with pliers. Make sure the blank takes the contours of the steel-spoon mould along its entire length from hole to hole.

8. Attach a treble hook with single or double split rings or wire loops. Attach a second split ring or wire loop to the front hole to tie up to.
9. Done. You can fish it as is, or add a pattern with paint or tape.

Alternatively, forget about moulding the blank. Fish it as a flat slab spoon or with a slight 'Z' bend along the axis. I usually leave the spoon flat and unbent until I go fishing. I test it first in the water, then bend it until it has the action I want.

In my experience, the moulded variety works best in very slow currents or at slow speeds, while the flat or 'Z'-bend variety works best in heavier currents or at faster speeds.

Note: these spoons are not nearly as tough and resilient as shop-bought examples. Just like home-made soft metal spoons, they bend easily when snagged or playing a fish. I always carry a number of back-ups. I take the badly bent ones back to my workshop and reshape them for later use.

Blade Spinners

Making a steel-bladed spinner that spins reliably in a range of currents and at different speeds is difficult to do from scratch. The easiest and commonest alternative to buying retail is purchasing components and assembling them yourself. Plenty of mail-order companies supply all the parts you need for making spinners. Start with Glasgow Angling Centre or Cabela's for Mepps-like spinners, and YGA's online store for the parts for making Flying C's:

Glasgow Angling Centre, online store only. (www.fishingmegastore.com)

Cabela's, online store only. (www.cabelas.com)

YGA (Yorkshire Game Angling), online store only. (www.yga.yorks.com)

Minnows

Wholesalers also sell components for assembling Devon-like minnows yourself. But it's also fairly easy to make reliable minnows from scratch.

MATERIALS:

For the body:
    Fine-tooth wood saw/steel hacksaw
    Stationary drill or wood lathe and hand drill
    Drill bits in sizes 3–6 mm
    Vice
    Sandpaper
    Sheet-metal cutters/tin snips
    Wooden dowels for minnow bodies in sizes ⅜ in (9 mm) to
        1 in (24 mm) diameter. Buy them or use old broom handles
        or the like.
    Tin-can metal for minnow fins
    Wood oil or sealant
    Superglue
    Wood primer and paints

For the hook mount:
    Plastic/wooden beads
    Ball-bearing swivels
    Treble hooks in sizes 6 to 2
    Heavy *c.* 20 lb (9 kg) test mono
    c. 1 mm diameter wire (copper, aluminium, steel will do)

MAKING THE BODY:

1. Cut wooden dowel to length.
2. Shape body. (If you've got a lathe, shape the body before you drill it. Give it a graceful 'cigar' or similar shape. Then smooth it with sandpaper. If you don't have a lathe, drill the body first: step 3.)
3. Drill the body. Bore a hole lengthwise through it with a stationary drill. Now leave it on the drill bit, so you can use the

drill as a vertical lathe. Shape the body with a knife or wood chisel to graceful 'cigar' or similar form. Remove from the drill.

4. Place the body in the vice and cut two wing slits on opposite sides of the body at about a 45° angle. If you want more wobble in the lure, place the slits forward (say a quarter of the way back); if you want less wobble place them up to halfway back.

5. Cut two fins from tin-can metal and glue into the slots. Make them bigger for faster spin, smaller for slower spin; experiment with size and shapes to see which work best for the currents you fish.

6. Paint the whole thing first with a wood oil or sealant, especially the inside of the hole; prime the outside; paint your pattern.

MOUNTING THE HOOK:

I use either wire or monofilament to rig up the hook trace: mono if I want a little more buoyancy, wire for a little less. For either, attach wire or mono first to the eye of the treble hook. Then string on two small beads – a little bigger than the diameter of the hole running through the minnow body. Now push the trace through the body and attach it to a small ball-bearing swivel. Make the trace long enough so the swivel just peeks out from the nose of the body. To hold the trace in place when it's not in use, you can slide a paper clip into the front swivel eye.

TUNING:

You might want to tune your minnow, once you've watched it perform in the water. Minnows tend to spin faster than you want in a salmon lure. To slow down the spin you can either shorten one or both wings by trimming with tin snips, or bend one or both wings back with pliers. You can do the same to reduce or enhance wobble in the lure. I like to tune mine so it has a slow wobbling spin.

Diving Plugs

A really good diving plug with reliable action is a high-tech piece of machinery with very narrow design tolerances. For the do-ityourselfer, this translates to hard work. I've tried making all kinds from scratch. In my estimation, the only design worth the effort is the J-plug/Kynock Killer variety. Even these require some water testing and heavy tuning to get them running as they should. But if you are up for a challenge, here's the basic recipe.

MATERIALS:

For the body:
    Fine-tooth wood saw
    Hand drill with *c.* 2.5 mm bit
    Vice
    Wood file or rasp with round or curved working face
    Sandpaper
    Wooden dowels for plug bodies in sizes ⅜ in (9 mm) to 1 in
        (25 mm) diameter. Buy them, or use old broom handles or
        the like.
    Wood oil or sealant
    Wood primer and paints

For the hook mount:
    Plastic/wooden beads
    Ball-bearing swivels
    Treble hooks in sizes 6 to 2
    Heavy *c.* 20 lb (9 kg) test mono
    c. 1 mm diameter wire (copper, aluminium, steel will do)

MAKING THE BODY:

1. Cut the dowel to length. Try different length-to-diameter proportions. Commercial J-plugs have dimensions of approximately
   5:1. Longer proportions tend to make for narrower actions; wider
   proportions, wider actions.
2. Give the body a graceful tapered shape using a wood file; sand
   it smooth.
3. Place the body in the vice and cut the head of the plug (wider
   end) off at about a 45° angle.
4. Drill a hole in the centre, perpendicular to the cut face through

and outside. The hole should end up about a quarter to a third of the way down the side from the head of the plug.

5. Using a wood rasp, put a slight concavity along the bevelled head.
6. Brush on wood oil or sealant (first treatment). Make sure you get it inside the drilled hole.
7. After tuning (see below) and final oil treatment, paint the pattern.

MOUNTING THE HOOK:

1. Make a hook mount from either wire or heavy monofilament. Mono makes for a more buoyant lure, wire less so. A wire mount allows for last-minute tuning.
2. Attach the wire or mono to the treble hook eye; string one or two beads on the line above the hook and run the wire or mono (trace) through the body. By adding beads or making knots in the mono you can adjust how far back the treble runs off the plug. You can also run one treble tight against the body and a second further back off the same trace. I generally run one treble far enough back so the point of the hook reaches the end of the plug. But watch that the barb tip doesn't catch on the tail of the plug.
3. Attach the trace to a barrel swivel ahead of the plug. If you are using a wire trace, place the swivel within 1 in (2.5 cm) of the bevelled plug head for attaching your mono. If you are using a mono trace you can do the same, or forget the extra swivel and run the trace right up to the swivel on the main line as your leader.

TUNING:

Unless you're charmed, you'll need to spend a little time on the water tuning your plugs. To do this you'll need your rod and reel and a wood rasp. I usually anchor my boat out in the current as if fishing, but you can work from land if the current is strong enough for a representative test. Drop the lure into the current and watch its action. Generally, the problem is getting the plug to track straight, rather than listing, running over on its side, or even spinning. If it's only listing a little and you've rigged it with a wire trace, try bending the trace in the direction of the list. If that doesn't straighten it out you'll need to file off some of the bevel with the rasp. Try filing down on the side toward the list. In my experience you'll need to do this a few times to get it tracking right. You can also try filing down one side of the tail section of the body. If you are lucky, you'll get most of the plugs you've made into good running order. If not, you may end up taking most back to the workshop for a complete reshaping. I usually end up throwing a certain proportion of mine away. With any plug whose body you tuned by filing, it's important to remember to let it dry and re-oil it before you prime and paint it for service.

Notes

1. I find it instructive to keep track of how many salmon are caught by different methods on some of the better-known rivers. For example, the Spey reported the following salmon catches for 2005 to 2008: 538 (34%) on fly; 362 (23%) on worm; 680 (43%) on spinner (see Strathspey Angling Improvement Association).
2. Bickerdyke stated: 'Spinning baits are either cast out some distance, and drawn back through the water to the angler, or trailed at the back of a boat.' Falkus (1984, pp. 323–6) also gave a brief history of the development of spinning tackle.
3. Anybody interested in stillwater salmon fishing should take a look at Falkus (1984), chap. XVII, and at McEwan.
4. These are the odds commonly tossed around by anglers. They were probably started by Falkus (1984). How accurate they are nobody can say – they could be much better, or much worse. More likely, it varies a lot.
5. Researchers measured maximum burst speeds for salmon (*Salmo salar*) at 13½ ft (4.13 m)/sec in 50°F (10°C) water (see Colavecchia *et al.*).
6. Commercial fisheries aim at ideal temperatures of 50–53°F (10°–12°C) for farming salmon (see Shaw and Muir); for wild breeding populations ideal spawning temperatures are 47–51°F (8.3°–10.5°C) (Armstrong *et al.*).
7. For a detailed description of habitat requirements for spawning and rearing young salmon, take a look at Armstrong *et al.*
8. One study among wild redds in the Burrishoole, western Ireland, system, showed about a 29% contribution to fertilization, a similar percentage to that found in other waters (see C.E. Thompson *et al.*).
9. John Bailey has written up the story of this famous catch in *Salmon Fishing: In Search of Silver*, pp. 124–6.
10. For mentions of early spin-baits see also Walton; Otter; Burgess; Kirkbride; Fitzgibbon; Daniel; Jacob.
11. One study of pooled field data suggests that, once a salmon reaches about 20 in (50 cm) in length, its diet is almost exclusively fish, with a preferred size of 2–4 in (5–10 cm). As it grows bigger, it targets even larger prey. So a fish of 40 in (1 m) will go for prey fish of about 6 in (15 cm) or larger! (see Keeley and Grant).
12. The evidence for red/orange as attractor colours is stronger for trout. A study of cutthroat and Dolly Varden trout showed that reaction distance

was greatest for red-sided prey (see Henderson and Northcote). Another, by Semler, showed that rainbows were more likely to attack sticklebacks with red throats than those without. Taylor reports trout's preference for trolled flies with red in them, and for red lures when ice fishing.

13. On the question of salmonid colour vision, the following are helpful: Tsin and Beatty; Cristy; Allen and McFarland. On vision in fish, including salmon, see Wallbridge; Kageyama.

14. Research seems to show that these changes correlate with temperature, light or developmental transitions like spawning migrations (see Flamarique).

15. Vogel and Beauchamp looked at the reaction distances (size of strike zone) of adult lake trout (char) to large prey fish at different light levels ranging from midday (100 lx) to night-time (0.17 lx). As light died down to night-time levels, reaction distances shrank by about 75% or to about 10 in (25 cm). However, greatest reaction distances – about 40 in (1 m) on average – were not under full daylight conditions, but at light levels closer to those experienced at early dusk, late dawn or under a darkly clouded sky (17.8 lx).

16. How quickly these changes occur is uncertain. Estimates range from several minutes to several hours (see Douglas and Djamoz; Wallbridge; Garth.

17. I found the following helpful in sorting out the colour-visibility issue: Frederick; Aprill; Lumb; Gibbs; also the section on colour penetration in Taylor.

18. Bash *et al.*; Sweka and Hartman.

19. Steelhead fishers like Bill Herzog use a similar system for steelhead. Spoon enthusiasts might want to look at his book *Spoon Fishing for Steelhead*.

20. These include those I called 'drifting spoons' in *Spin-Fishing for Sea Trout*.

21. These include those I called 'swimming spoons' in *Spin-Fishing for Sea Trout*.

22. There is some evidence from older writings that the problem of poor hook-ups with spoons goes back much further. In 1867 Burgess wrote (p. 92) that 'The spoon bait is still used in many sizes in different localities. The present mode of using it appears defective, and the plan of adding a flying triangle [treble-hook] at the side would probably add to its efficiency.'

23. Mark Zinzer of FishinMission Guide Service recommends replacing the stock siwash hook that comes on some lures with a 1/0 or a 2/0 treble hook of your choice.

24. In one study Vogel and Beauchamp used underwater filming to show that under ideal water and light conditions adult lake trout (char) struck large prey fish (rainbow and cutthroat trout, from 2–5½ in (5.5–14 cm) when they were within about 6 ft (1.8 m), on average about 3 ft (1m).

25. Anglers trolling for feeding salmon seem to assume a greater reaction distance. Scandinavian pros put it at up to 10 ft (3 m) (see Regal Sport-

fiskes Trollingskola). As already noted Dick Pool felt you could draw a salmon in from as far as 30 ft (9 m). But these are for clear, stillwater conditions.

26. See reports by Newcombe; Sweka and Hartman; Barrett *et al.*; Berg and Northcote.

27. I was surprised to find that there has been precious little done in the way of scientific research on the question of running depths of salmon. My current understanding comes from anglers' observations (my own included), along with the observations of a number of fish biologists kind enough to correspond with me. These include Jon Svedsen, Morten Stickler, Petri Karppinen, Panu Orell, Saija Koljonen; Peter Rivinoja; Frode Oppedal, Eva B. Thorstad, Eli Kvingedal. I also got hold of a few relevant studies, including Thorstad *et al.*; Akita *et al.*; Makiguchi *et al.*

28. Experienced stillwater anglers troll for feeding salmon at similar speeds of 2–2½ mph (3–4 kmph). Some, like Dick Pool, feel keeping your lure fishing with the right action counts more for success than its speed *per se*. But he concedes that most lures he uses perform best when trolled at speeds of 2–2½ mph (3–4 kmph).

29. If we consider how fish ladders are designed, we can probably assume a salmon's maximum burst speed will drop by about 50% once water has dropped to 42°F (5°C) (see Croft). That's down to about 5 ft (1.5 m) per second (see Croft).

30. Bill Herzog touted the advantages of bottom-bouncing for steelhead. He called it 'ringing the dinner bell'.

31. Scuba divers periodically scour the bottom of the more heavily fished beats for lost lures, and they seem to recover most of them. Some of mine have come back to me several times!

32. Several companies including Abu, Shimano, Penn and Fladen make fixed-spool reels that will give line freely (with the bail-arm closed) by simply flicking a lever. These are called bait-runners, free-liners or similar.

33. From a letter of 30 July 2007.

34. Fishing and making wake flies are discussed in Falkus (1983) and my *Spin-Fishing for Sea Trout*.

35. Falkus sometimes drift-jigged a small, heavy tube fly – Dee Special Nymph – which he felt was an effective way to hook a vacillating 'Hamlet' fish (Falkus 1984, p. 308).

36. Falkus seemed to anticipate the effectiveness of this kind of presentation which he called 'Overhead fishing', 'in which a specially designed lure is cast so that it drops vertically into a salmon's lie' (1984, p. 58). He was right!

37. Falkus (1984, p. 336) recommended the following breaking strains for mono spinning leaders: 20–25 lb (9–11 kg) for early spring fishing with a multiplier reel; 16–20 lb (7–9 kg) for early spring fishing with a fixed-spool reel; 12–15 lb (5.5–7 kg) for general spinning with a fixed-spool reel; 10–12 lb (4.5–5.5 kg) for low-water summer fishing with a fixed-spool reel.

38. For additional tips on float methods, the following are helpful: Carrao; Peck; and Kaye.
39. Fishing guide Vic Carrao described these.
40. These early methods are briefly described in O'Gorman, pp. 55–9; Francis, p. 9; Williamson, p. 170–1.
41. I'm learning to use a drift anchor to brake my boat's speed when back trolling. I've tried several types including cannonball, disc, claw, chain, even a cinder block.

   So far, chain works best for me: about 10 ft (3 m) of very heavy logging chain tied to the end of my regular anchor line. The key is getting the drag just right, and I'm learning to regulate it by letting more or less chain drag along the bottom. When I get this right it works nicely: the boat backs down the river slowly, and I sit in the stern (facing downriver) and concentrate on bouncing my hardware along the bottom. The chain does catch on the bottom occasionally, but much less than with other anchors I've tried. Noise is a problem, when I lift the chain or lower it over the side, but padding should tame that.

   A word of caution though. If you stand up in the boat when playing a fish, watch out when using a drift anchor. Even the best catch the bottom now and then, and then the boat lurches to a stop; if you're standing in the stern when it does, you'll probably get wet! I speak from experience!
42. A few companies make fused braid lines that ice up a lot less than normal braid. Cortland's braided Ice line is a good one.
43. Believe it or not, once water get colder than 40°F (4°C), it gets lighter! This means that in freezing temperatures the water at the bottom of a pool can actually be a little warmer than the water above it.
44. This advice comes from Fish Sponge and Contributing Authors.
45. Hugh Falkus (1984, pp. 14–21; 293) made the point that you can't over-fish a lie provided you don't frighten the fish. He championed dogging a single fish by covering it over and over again until it finally takes.
46. That boat traffic can improve salmon fishing conditions was noted by anglers at Fish Sponge and Contributing Authors.
47. Experienced anglers trolling still waters for feeding salmon in Scandinavia also consider water from 45–50°F (7–10°C) ideal for taking fish (see Regal Sportfiskes Trollingskola).
48. All glow-in-the-dark finishes or lure materials require recharging, usually every ten minutes or so, by illuminating them. Some brands can hold a charge longer. Experienced glow-baiters use a flash-box with reflective interiors that they put the lure into and hold a light on.
49. Some rivers are off limits for night fishing, the better to detect poachers, who usually operate under the cloak of darkness.

Bibliography

Akita, M., Y. Makiguchi, H. Nii, K. Nakao, J.F. Sandahl and H. Ueda, 'Upstream migration of chum salmon through a restored segment of the Shibetsu River', *Ecology of Freshwater Fish*, vol. 15, 2006, pp. 125–30.

Allen, D. M. and W.N. McFarland, 'Effect of temperature on rhodopsin-porphyropsin ratios in a fish', *Vision Research*, vol. 13, 1973, pp. 1303–09.

Aprill, D., 'Certain colors are really fishy', *Plattsburgh (NY) Press-Republican*, 13 July 2003.

Armstrong, J.D., P.S. Kemp, G.J.A. Kennedy, M. Ladle and N.J. Milner, 'Habitat requirements of Atlantic Salmon and Brown Trout in rivers and streams', *Fisheries Research*, vol. 62, 2003, pp. 143–70.

Bailey, J., *Salmon Fishing: In Search of Silver*, Marlborough: Crowood Press, 1994.

Barrett, J. D., G. D. Grossman and J. Risenfeld, 'Turbidity-induced changes in reaction distance in rainbow trout', *Transactions of the American Fisheries Society*, vol. 121, 1992, pp. 437–43.

Bash, J., C. Berman and S. Balton, *Effects of Turbidity and Suspended Solids on Salmonids*, Seattle: Centre for Streamside Studies, University of Washington, 2001.

Berg, L.S, and T.G. Northcote, 'Changes in territorial, gill-flaring, and feeding behavior in juvenile Coho salmon (*Oncorynchus kisutch*) following short impulses of suspended sediments', *Canadian Journal of Fisheries and Aquatic Sciences*, vol. 42, 1985, pp.1410–17.

Bickerdyke, J., *The Book of the All Round Angler*, London: L. Gill 1888.

Burgess, J.T., *Angling: A Practical Guide to Bottom Fishing, Trolling, Spinning and Fly-Fishing*, London: Frederick Warne, 1867.

Carrao V., 'Floats 'n Spinners' (www.guidebc.com, consulted 1 October 2009).

Central Fisheries Board (www.cfb.ie/publications/index.htm, consulted 1 October 2009)

Cholmondeley-Pennell, H., *The Book of the Pike: A Practical Treatise on the Various Methods of Jack Fishing; with an Analysis of the Tackle Employed, the History of the Fish, etc. Also a Chapter on Spinning for Trout in Lakes and Rivers.* London: R. Hardwicke, 1865.

Colavecchia, M., C. Katopodis, R. Goosney, D.A. Scruton and R.S. McKinley, 'Measurement of burst swimming performance in wild Atlantic salmon (*Salmo salar L.*) using digital telemetry in Regulated Rivers', *Research Management*, vol. 14, no. 1, 1998, pp. 41–5.

Cristy M., 'Effects of temperature and light intensity on the visual pigments of rainbow trout', *Vision Research*, vol. 16, no. 11, 1976, pp. 1225–8.

Croft, D., *Fish Ladder Design*, Croft Consultants, 2000.

Dahl, J., J. Dannewitz, L. Karlsson, E. Petersson, A. Löf and B. Ragnarsson, 'Timing of spawning migration: implications of environmental variation, life history, and sex', *Canadian Journal of Zoology*, vol. 82, no. 12, 2004, pp. 1864–70.

Daniel, W. B. (ed.), *Rural Sports*, London: Longman, Hurst, Rees & Orme, 1812.

Douglas, R. H., and M.B.A. Djamoz, *The Visual System of Fish*, London: Chapman and Hall, 1990.

Falkus, H., *Sea Trout Fishing*, London: Witherby, 1983.

——— *Salmon Fishing*, London: Witherby, 1984.

Finstad, A.G., F. Økland, E.B. Thorstad and T.G. Heggberget, 'Comparing upriver spawning migration of Atlantic salmon (*Salmo salar*) and sea trout (*Salmo trutta*)', *Journal of Fish Biology*, vol. 67, 2005, pp. 919–30.

Fitzgibbon, E., *A Handbook of Angling teaching Fly-fishing, Trolling, Bottom-fishing and Salmon-fishing*, London: Longmans Green, 1865.

Fish Sponge and Contributing Authors, 'Steelhead & Salmon 1-Oh!-1' (www.fishsponge.com/Tips.htm, consulted 6 October 2009).

Flamarique, I.N., 'Temporal shifts in visual pigment absorbance in the retina of Pacific salmon', *Journal of Comparative Physiology A: Sensory, Neural, and Behavioral Physiology*, vol. 191, no. 1, 2005, pp. 37–49.

Francis, F., *A Book on Angling, Being a Complete Treatise on the Art of Angling in Every Branch*, London: Longmans, Green, and Co., 1867.

Frederick, L., 'How to select lure colours for successful fishing', University of Wisconsin Sea Grant Institute, 2001.

Gage M., P. Stockley and G.A. Parker, 'Effects of alternative male mating strategies on characteristics of sperm production in the Atlantic Salmon (*Salmo salar*): Theoretical and Empirical Investigations', *Philosophical Transactions: Biological Sciences*, vol. 350, no. 1334, 1995, pp. 391–9.

Garth, M., 'Colour in the Fishes Eye'(www.sexyloops.com/articles/colourinthefisheseye.shtml, consulted 1 October 2009).

Gibbs, J., 'Visionary Angling' (www.outdoorlife.com, consulted 6 October 2009).

Henderson, M. A., and T. G. Northcote, 'Visual prey detection and foraging in sympatric cutthroat trout (*Salmo clarki clarki*) and Dolly Varden (*Salvelinus malma*)', *Canadian Journal of Fisheries and Aquatic Sciences*, vol. 42, 1985, pp. 785–90.

Herzog, B., *Spoon Fishing for Steelhead*, Portland OR: Frank Amato Publications, 1993.

Idler, D.R., U.H.M. Fagerlund and H. Mayoh, with the collaboration of J. R. Brett and D. F. Alderdice, 'Olfactory Perception in migrating salmon. I. L-Serine: a salmon repellent in mammalian skin', *Journal of General Physiology*, vol. 39, 1956, pp. 889–92.

Jacob, G., *The Compleat Sportsman*, London: J. Jonson and W. Taylor, 1718.

Juell, J., and J.E. Fosseidengen, 'Use of artificial light to control swimming depth and fish density of Atlantic salmon (*Salmo salar*) in production cages', Institute of Marine Research, Matredal N-5984, 2003.

Kadri, S., Thorpe J.E., Metcalfe N.B., 'Anorexia in one-sea-winter Atlantic salmon (*Salmo salar*) during summer, associated with sexual maturation', *Aquaculture*, vol. 151, no. 1, 1997, pp. 405–9.

Kageyama, C. J., *What Fish See: Understanding Optics and Color Shifts for Designing Lures and Flies*, Portland OR: Frank Amato Publications, 1999.

Karppinen, P., J. Erkinaro, E. Niemelä, K. Moen and F. Økland, 'Return migration of one-sea-winter Atlantic salmon in the River Tana', *Journal of Fish Biology*, vol. 64, no. 5, 2004, pp. 1179–92.

Kaye, S., 'Strategies for autumn salmon fishing in the rivers of British Columbia, Canada', *BC Outdoors Sport Fishing*, September 2002.

Keeley, E., and J. Grant, 'Prey size of salmonid fishes in streams, lakes, and oceans', *Canadian Journal of Aquatic Sciences*, vol. 58, 2001, pp. 1122–32.

Kirkbride, J., *The Northern Angler; Or, Fly-fisher's Companion*, Carlisle: C. Thurnam, 1837.

Llewelyn, Lloyd, *Field Sports of the North of Europe: Comprised in a Personal Narrative of a Residence in Sweden and Norway, in the Years 1827–28* (2nd ed.), London: H. Colburn and R. Bentley, 1831.

Lumb, D., 'Lure Fishing in colored water' (www.muskiecentral.com, consulted 6 October 2009).

Makiguchi, Y., H. Nii, K. Nakao and H. Ueda, 'Upstream migration of adult chum and pink salmon in the Shibetsu River', *Hydrobiologia*, vol. 582, no. 1, 2007, pp. 43–54.

McEwan, B. *Angling on Lomond*, Edinburgh: Albyn Press, 1980.

Newcombe, C., Impact assessment model for clear water fishes exposed to excessively cloudy water', *Journal of the American Water Resources Association*, vol. 39, no. 3, 2003, pp. 529–44.

O'Gorman, J., *The Practice of Angling, Particularly as Regards Ireland*, Dublin: William Curry and Co., 1855.

Otter [Henry Jervis Alfred], *The Modern Angler – Containing instructions on the Art of Fly-fishing, Spinning and Bottom-fishing*, London: Alfred & Son, 1864.

Peck, J., 'Early Fall Salmon' (www.jaypeckguides.com, consulted 5 October 2009).

Pool, D., 'Salmon Fishing Techniques', (www.protroll.com, consulted 6 October 2009).

Regal Sportfiskes Trollingskola, 'Regal Sportfiske Fisketips'. (www.regalmarin.se, consulted 1 October 2009).

Semler, D., 'Some aspects of adaptation in a polymorphism for breeding colours in the threespine stickleback (*Gasterosteus aculeatus*)', *Journal of Zoology (London)*, vol. 165, 1971, pp. 291–302.

Shaw, S., and J. F. Muir. *Salmon: Economics and Marketing*, London: Croom Helm; Portland OR: Timber Press 1987.

Smith, G., *The Gentleman Angler*, London: A. Bettesworth, 1726.

Strathspey Angling Improvement Association (www.speyfishing-grantown.co.uk, consulted 1 October 2009).

Sweka, J. A., and K.J. Hartman, 'Effects of turbidity on prey consumption and growth in brook trout and implications for bioenergetics modeling', *Canadian Journal of Fisheries and Aquatic Sciences*, vol. 58, 2001, pp. 386–93.

Taylor, B., *Big Trout. How and Where to Target Trophies*, Guilford CT: Lyons Press, 2002.

Thompson, C.E., W.R. Poole, M.A. Matthews and A. Ferguson, 'Comparison, using minisatellite DNA profiling, of secondary male contribution in the fertilisation of wild and ranched Atlantic salmon (*Salmo salar*) ova', *Canadian Journal of Fisheries and Aquatic Sciences*, vol. 55, no. 9, 1998, pp. 2011–18.

Thompson, H., *The Spooners*, Dearborn, MI: Eppinger Manufacturing, 1979.

Thorstad, E.B., P. Fiske, K. Aarestrup, N.A. Hvidsten, K. Hårsaker, T.G. Heggberget and F. Økland, 'Upstream migration of Atlantic salmon in three regulated rivers', in M.T. Spedicato, G. Lembo and G. Marmulla (eds) *Aquatic telemetry: advances and applications* (Proceedings of the Fifth Conference on Fish Telemetry held in Europe, Ustica, Italy, 9–13 June 2003), Rome, FAO/COISPA, 2005.

Tsin, A.T., and D.D. Beatty, 'Visual pigment changes in rainbow trout in response to temperature', *Science*, vol. 95, no. 4284, 1977, pp. 1358–60.

Vogel, J. L., and D.A. Beauchamp, 'Effects of light, prey size, and turbidity on reaction distances of lake trout (*Salvelinus namaycush*) to salmonid prey', *Canadian Journal of Fisheries and Aquatic Sciences*, vol. 56, no. 7, 1999, pp. 1293–7.

Wallbridge, D., 'Fish Vision – and the Salmonids' (www.sexyloops.com/articles/whatsalmonidssee.shtml, consulted 6 October 2009).

Walton, I., *The Compleat Angler, Or the Contemplative Man's Recreation: Being a Discourse on Rivers, Fish-ponds, Fish, and Fishing*, with notes by Charles Cotton, John Hawkins, James Rennie. London: Fraser, 1836 (reprint of 1676 edition).

Webster, G., *Spin-Fishing for Sea Trout*, Ramsbury: Crowood Press, 2008.

Williamson, T., *The Complete Angler's Vade-Mecum*, London: Payne and Mackinlay, 1808.

Zinzer, M., FishinMission Guide Service (www.fishinmission.net, consulted 5 October 2009).

Index